From
Turmoil
to
Tranquility

From
Turmoil
to
Tranquility

Your
Step-By-Step Guide
To Total Emotional Freedom

Cindy Cooke, M. A.

Sundance Communications, International
8032 East Del Rubi
Scottsdale, Arizona   85258

First Edition, 2002
Manufactured in the United States of America

Applied for Library of Congress Cataloging-in-Publication Data
Cooke, Cindy
From Turmoil to Tranquility/Cindy Cooke
p.   cm.

1. Self-Help   2. Psychology   3. New Age
ISBN 0-971-43461-1

ATTENTION: Colleges, Universities, Professional Organizations and Corporations: Quantity discounts are available for educational purposes, fundraising or for gifts. For further information, call the Marketing Department at Sundance Communications, 480 367-1684

Comments and Kudo's

♦ ♦ ♦ ♦ ♦

When I went through the process I felt the electrical energy drain out of my system. That's how I felt. That's how I visualized it. This electricity is just flowing out of me. It was unbelievable. Almost immediately, I felt lighter. A thousand pounds lighter. Something had been released, and I wasn't quite sure what it was. I'm a new person. J. R., CFO

The process didn't take that long, maybe 20 minutes, but I ended up after that feeling cleaner, more secure, less afraid. It was such a different feeling. Everything looked clearer, like ah, wow, something had lifted off of me was the feeling. I really don't have any words to describe it. I feel a lot better now, and I feel like something was lifted. Whatever happened was important and I don't necessarily have to understand it. The main point is I feel better. A. S., Graduate Student

My feelings of anxiety and depression were lifted within probably a couple of days. I just didn't have that feeling that had been a part of my life for such long time. By the next day (after doing the process) when I woke up, I felt greatly relieved. I felt as though a tremendous burden had been lifted. And then for a long time after that I would just feel better each day and at more peace with myself. P. R., Small Business Owner

What a week this has been! I have been releasing on a non-stop basis. I brought the tapes home and my husband has listened to them and is releasing also. This is what we have been looking for for a long time. I breathe so much better than I ever have, it seems to be a deeper more satisfying breath. I also noticed that things that irritate me come up quicker than before, but instead of yelling at the person that supposedly "caused me to get angry", I quickly internalize the situation and feel it to the max, then release it. My husband picked up the technique right away also. In fact he said the release feels exactly like the big "O". Our home is much more peaceful, our relationship is improving every day. It was never a bad relationship, but now it is feeling like it did when we first fell in love. April 25th is our 21st wedding anniversary, I could not think of a better gift, than what we've received from this program. Thank you!! A. B., Homemaker

Other anonymous comments from seminar participants:

This has changed my life. I truly feel I can have a life filled with joy and peace. I am thrilled.

Wonderful! It will change your life forever.

I love the step by step process given. Great info – refreshing approach.

It got to the heart of the issue. I've tried a lot of things. This gave me the tools

Great new way to look at it. A chance of a lifetime to get a handle on life.

It took a very different approach and effective approach to healing the pain. It was great and will change my life.

Try it. It's different than anything that you might have tried to heal yourself. It's an eye opener. It gives very healthy advice.

It's great! Especially if you've tried everything else.

Excellent. Affects you physically (I no longer clench my teeth as often), emotionally and mentally. Just frees you up.

Contents

♦ ♦ ♦ ♦ ♦

PART III. THE PROCESS: How to Have an Emotional Orgasm: .
. . and Just Let Go – *the Six Steps to Serenity*

To Mildred Russell

Whose one year of unstinting motherly love

gave me the knowledge that there was a place of peace

and the courage to keep looking.

Without you, this book would not have been possible.

Introduction and Acknowledgments

◆ ◆ ◆ ◆ ◆

Recently, neuroscientists discovered an innate mechanism in a part of the brain called the amygdala that actually dissolves emotional trauma – *if you let it.* The actual break-up of emotional memories and distress can be seen with a sophisticated brain imaging technique called an fMRI. So, why isn't it working for you and other Americans, 48% of whom will experience a major emotional disorder at some time in their lives?

It is because we are confused about the functions of two critical parts of the brain – the rational or verbal brain and the emotional or sensate brain, how and when to use each. If you are catching a cold, or example, do you need to know the name of the germ or the intricacies of your immune system? Not at all. You need only to know that you are feeling ill and need to rest, need to drink more fluids, etc. The process is similar with emotional injury.

From Turmoil to Tranquility links the growth of emotional distress to our overwhelming and inappropriate reliance on verbal and intellectual abilities to do a job for which it is not biologically suited. It describes a far more powerful source of information, the ability to perceive, interpret, understand and know when to follow our most subtle physical sensations, and the central role this ability plays in producing not only emotional tranquility, but physical and spiritual health as well.

Using the latest brain research as a background, *From Turmoil to Tranquility* introduces the concept of Amygdala Deficit Disorder, a fundamental imbalance between two critical portions of the brain. It explains why this imbalance is at the core of the epidemic of not only the anxiety disorders and depression that is sweeping the globe today, but, as we will see, also the cause of most relationship difficulties, life crises, and social chaos as well. In addition, it documents how this imbalance contributes to the parallel epidemic of stress and immune disorders such as arthritis, heart disease, diabetes and obesity. It tells us why our most popular cures not only don't work, but why they *can't*.

Perhaps more importantly, it provides a cookbook-like prescription for redressing that balance and restoring our innate emotional immune system – a process that will restore us to full emotional health – *if we let it*.

I have included many stories from those who have attended my seminars, and have removed their names to protect their privacy. All such quotes appear in indented italics, and I am most grateful to these generous and brave souls who have given me permission to include their experiences.

I strongly recommend that you read this book in its entirety before embarking on any of the specific prescriptions for emotional freedom that are included in Part III. While that section does include specific steps to dissolve emotional distress, you *must* understand the principles of the emotional brain to understand the actual changes that will be taking place in your body as you release old emotional memories. Otherwise you may become confused by your sensations, misinterpret them, think you are doing something wrong, and abandon the effort. Parts I and II of the book are designed to help you take a broader view of your emotional distress, understand where it came from and provide the principles that will help you grasp – in the broader and deeper sense – how to live distress-free for the rest of your life.

From Turmoil to Tranquility has been a project of joy and frustration: joy to be able to share my experience for the benefit of others . . . frustration because my mind just does not think in a linear fashion, and, alas, that is the only way a book can be written!

I want to thank the many people who made this book possible

- ◆ My parents – though they may not have given me what I needed as a child to be healthy and whole, they did the very best job they could. And, because they did a far better job than many, I was able to finally emerge from the emotional turmoil with a love for life and a full appreciation of the banquet it offers.

- ◆ My beautiful daughter Beth, who, because of her belief in feelings and force of personality has stopped the spread of the emotional distress that infected our family. To her loving husband Mike, for his support of her, and my grandson Kyle (with another – to be named Conner? – on the way). They will be the first generation in our immediate family to grow up knowing who they are and finding joy in their place in the world.

- ◆ My attorney and friend, John Noel, for his legal brilliance, steadfast loyalty, impeccable ethics, and brotherly love, for giving me an unprecedented view of what it is to care about another human being without expecting anything from them. And his lovely wife Sara, who endured tremendous sacrifices, bore it all with grace, style and wit, and kept her husband's spirits up when he worked for years on my behalf without recompense.

- ◆ All the angels in my life – those who caused pain (you probably know who you are, so I won't name you here) as well as to those who did not, including my dear friend, Sally Fleer; my writing and psychology guru, Brian Gerrard; my major Professor at ASU, Roger Axford; my nephews Jeff Cooke who warmly welcomed me to the Cooke family, and Jim Cooke who worked long and hard on my website; Anna Sherwood, a program graduate and the person who took over the website and runs it now.

♦ My many friends including Alec Bigelson, Bill Gerard, Kraig Kelly, Karen Lanier, Bill Russell, and many others who took the time to read parts of the manuscript and give me an honest critique.

♦ A special thanks to editor Gabriella Harvey, an editor who made much needed suggestions, each of which I followed religiously; and to Kerby Lecka and Joe Cibere from Westlake Marketing Works for all their advice and hard work.

♦ All the wonderful students who participated in *Turmoil to Tranquility* seminars, who let me experiment and gave constructive feedback that helped me strengthen the material and clarify my ideas.

I would also like to invite all of you who read this book to contact me with your stories through my website, TherapistWithin.com or MentalMakeovers.com and let me know - what worked for you? What is your history, and how did you come upon the book, and what else would you like to know?

May you have a successful journey back to yourself.

Nature is the physician;
we, only her assistants

Galen

From Turmoil to Tranquility

PART I
The Problem

You're Not Stupid
and You're Not Weak

*Why the Smart and the Strong
Are the Last to "Get It"*

PART 1:

Prologue

The Amygdala

You Are Not Alone

Lookin' for Help in All the Wrong Places

Mother Nature's Miracle Medicine

Prologue

♦　♦　♦　♦　♦

First there was fear. Then there was everything else. Everything else was my trying to escape the fear, to keep it in check and survive. Occasionally, tranquility descended like a fragile, pale butterfly alighting ever so tentatively on my shoulder while I held my breath, desperately trying to prolong a moment of peace. But inevitably, without notice or rationale, it flew away and "the terrors" descended again.

I spent the first half of my life battling the raging anxiety that bore down and sucked me up like a tornado. In and out of foster homes from birth to the age of seven, I had a mother given to hurling butcher knives in my direction and a politician father who chose not to bequeath me his name nor tell his wife or family of my existence. Escaping at eighteen, I married an intensely unhappy, violent musician whose idea of love was to throw a can of beer in my face when I reached for his hand and whose concept of responsibility included leaving our baby at the auto mechanic while he visited a prostitute and paid her with a check from our joint checking account.

Though I divorced him after seven brutal years and created with my daughter what would be considered by outsiders to be a "good life," I was always fearful, petrified that "the bottom would fall out." And, while I pursued every psychological trick I knew, panic was my partner in planes, tunnels, bridges, elevators, and skyscrapers, in relationships, and in business. During the day, I distracted myself with work, frenetic activity, and obsessive thoughts, and at night I slept fitfully, awakening all too frequently as if to guard against some imminent ominous threat. There was no reprieve. Anxiety accompanied me awake or asleep. Day after day, I battled the emotional rapids, trying to keep myself afloat, to keep from being dragged under and drowning, struggling to save myself from the precipice of a great fall and what I was sure would be certain disaster.

And then, when I thought it could get no worse, there was Russia.

CHAPTER 1

♦ ♦ ♦ ♦ ♦

The Amygdala:
The Mind/Body/Spirit Connection

What lies before us and what lies beyond us is tiny compared to what lies within us.   *Oliver Wendell Holmes*

O f all our capabilities, intelligence is perhaps the one in which we have the most pride. The very name given man – homosapiens – means "thinking man." When biologists refer to our "higher capacities" they are talking about the characteristic that separates man from animals – the capacity to think rationally and solve problems, the portion of the brain that is under man's control.

> Logic: The art of thinking and reasoning in strict accordance with the limitations and incapacities of the human misunderstanding.
> —*Ambrose Bierce*

So it is perhaps understandable that when most of us contemplate "the brain," we think only about using logic, or "figuring things out." We use phrases like "use your brain," or "going out of your mind," phrases that equate the brain with *thought*, a function that occurs in a part of the brain called the neocortex.

But the neocortex, actually a thin coating no more than ¼ inch thick is both more limited in its functions and less responsible for our happiness and success than most of us believe.

Similar to a computer that generates alternatives and choices, the neocortex does not even produce those "rational" decisions of which we are all so proud. In fact, Daniel Goleman, author of *Emotional Intelligence* estimates that only 10% to 20% of our success is due to IQ. The rest, he believes, is due to luck and "Emotional Intelligence" (EQ), a skill that rests in a different part of the brain.

Amygdala Deficit Disorder

Take a look at the list of symptoms on the next page. Which of them apply to you? If you are like most people in emotional distress, you may suffer from many of them. It is not uncommon to have more than a dozen of these symptoms because they all come from a disorder of a part of the brain you (and your therapist) may never have heard of, the emotional brain, or amygdala.

Until the development of new brain imaging techniques such as fMRIs which take a moving picture of the brain, emotion was simply too difficult to study scientifically. Psychology has preferred to study behavior or cognitive (information processing) functions and most therapists have focused their attention on how to use the rational brain to control a disturbed emotional brain rather than attacking the problem directly.

But now, thanks to the research of neuroscientists such as Joseph LeDoux and Antonio Damasio we have a glimpse of the nature, source, structure and process of emotion. While there are a number

Symptoms of Amygdala Deficit Disorder

♦ Phobias, anxiety attacks, post traumatic stress disorder, obsessive compulsive disorder, persistent depression, or attacks of anger.

♦ Trouble with boundaries, having other people take advantage of or manipulate you.

♦ Confusion about the difference between thoughts and feelings or being unsure where feelings are located.

♦ Not knowing the difference between being valued for who you are vs what you do.

♦ Being unaware of intuitive sensations or habitually overruling them.

♦ Recurrent life crises, especially in the area of relationships, jobs, or money.

♦ The voices and expectations of others are louder than your internal ones.

♦ Confusion regarding the meaning of the terms self, soul, inner spirit, the feeling that life has no meaning.

♦ Feelings that change from day to day or confusion about what you feel.

♦ Obsessive thoughts that can sometimes keep you awake at night.

♦ The desire to "let go" but not knowing how. The need to control – other people, other circumstances, yourself.

♦ Difficulty being completely open and honest with others.

♦ Difficulty making decisions.

♦ Needing to hold on tight or fearing that it will all fall apart.

♦ Feeling the weight of the world on your shoulders.

♦ Addictions to any substance, or mood-altering medications.

♦ The need for external symbols of success to be content and happy.

♦ Avoiding unpleasant tasks or issues.

♦ Wanting to know what is normal, how others behave.

♦ Difficulty staying motivated.

♦ The sense that you need to control or subdue your feelings.

♦ The belief that other people cause you emotional turmoil.

of structures involved in emotion, the amygdala appears to play the more dominant role, especially in the development of fear and anxiety, so that is where we will focus most of our attention in the pages ahead.[1]

The More Critical Tasks

Though far less well-known than the neocortex, the amygdala (pronounced ah-*mig*-dah-lah), a finger-nail sized, almond shaped structure buried deep in the skull, requires more brain structures and systems; its functions are more complex, interconnected, and the implications more critical to our well-being than the neocortex.

> Cognitive science treats minds like computers and has traditionally been more interested in how people and machines solve logical problems or play chess than in why we are sometimes happy and sometimes sad.
> —*Joseph LeDoux*

The amygdala, (there are actually two of them, one on each side of the brain) not the neocortex has the primary responsibility for our emotional tranquility and, as we will see, contributes substantially to our physical health and spiritual contentment as well. The amygdala is, in essence, the genius of Mother Nature. Its purpose is no less than to keep us healthy, whole, joyful, and *alive*. It is designed to:

♦ **Save our lives.** The amygdala is our internal guardian angel, the source of our instincts and intuition. Like an alert sentry, the amygdala is on guard, continually evaluating the environment in terms of its benefit or danger to us and signaling pre-programmed responses that help us thrive, survive, prevail or escape. The amygdala is the source of the "fight or flight" response, and its function is to keep us – and other animals – safe. Its role is critical to our survival. Arthur Kling from the University of Chicago reports that within seven

---

[1] *There are many interdependencies within the brain that I have chosen not to describe in this book because I am sure most of you are more interested in relieving emotional distress than embarking on an advanced course in brain structure and processes. The functions I have described, while not isolated in the amygdala are generally centered there.*

hours of releasing seven monkeys with amygdala lesions into the wild, all but one had vanished to predators.

♦ **Provide essential guidance and enrichment :** The amygdala is the source of our emotions. A component of instincts, emotions, such as fear, anger, sadness or delight, is the name we give to groups of physical sensations that are either pleasant or unpleasant. Unlike behavior that can be right or wrong, emotions are *never* wrong. They are messages from Mother Nature that contain vital information and directions that, if followed, will help ensure our well-being. *Emotions happen **to** us, they are not something we **do**.*

♦ **Store our emotional memories.** The amygdala enables us to fear those things that are painful, dangerous and may cause us harm so that we can avoid them in the future. Though the emotions themselves are stored in the amygdala via a protein synthesis, facts surrounding the emotions are stored elsewhere, in the hippocampus and neocortex.   If you were frightened by a bee as a child, for example, the fear itself is stored in the amygdala. The fact that it was a sunny day, that you were in the backyard by your tree house, however, is stored elsewhere. As we will see in the next part of the book, this dual storage process makes it possible to dissolve emotional memories without disturbing factual ones.

♦ **Answer the question: Who am I? And why am I here?** The amygdala is the source of meaning and direction. It is what draws us to some activities – makes us prefer music or numbers to art, for example and, in so doing, tells us our place and importance in the universe. Life without the amygdala, according to studies that have been done on those in whom it has been surgically removed, is a life stripped of meaning and direction. It is a life without knowing why you are here or who you are supposed to be. The amygdala is the origin of our sense of purpose in the larger universe, and the foundation of genuine and lasting self-confidence.

◆ **Provide the feelings that allow us to form meaningful relationships:** The amygdala is the source of our connection to others, enables us to have meaningful relationships, and to appreciate the contributions of our fellow human beings. In cases where the amygdala has been removed or damaged, patients may recognize family and friends, but ignore them.

> All that is worth cherishing in this world begins in the heart, not the head.
> —Suzanne Chazin

The importance of the relationship has been lost. A stranger or hospital worker has the same level of meaningfulness to the patient as does their spouse or child. Sadly, interactions with *things* are as interesting as those with *people*.

◆ **Enable us to make efficient decisions in keeping with our purpose:** Like the sort function on a computer, the amygdala puts the alternatives that are generated in the neocortex in priority order, allowing us to value and choose one over the other. It is the amygdala that allows us to make decisions, not the rational neocortex as most would have us believe.

Goleman tells the story of Elliot, once a successful lawyer. Though every bit as intelligent after brain surgery that severed the connections between the amygdala and neocortex, Elliot was unable to make a decision, even one as mundane as when to make his next appointment with the therapist. Every option was neutral to him. Though able to list the pros and cons of each, he was unable to assign different values to each and therefore unable to choose.

The emotional brain or amygdala, in summary, is responsible for a family of related and critical functions that are in short supply in the emotionally distressed.

> Your vision will become clear only when you look into your heart. Who looks outside, dreams. Who looks inside, awakens.
> —Carl Jung

The More Powerful Structure

But it is not only that nature has given the amygdala more important tasks than it has given the neocortex. It has also made this part of the brain far more powerful and more likely to prevail.

♦ **Feelings are faster than thoughts.** Because the amygdala reacts faster to environmental cues than the neocortex, emotions typically occur before thoughts. While thoughts can *influence* our feelings, can dampen and delay them a bit, it is a biological impossibility for thoughts to completely *control* feelings in the long-run. This is why, though therapies that rely on the rational brain to control the emotional brain – talk therapy, cognitive therapy and the like – may work in the short run, they generally produce only minor, short term results.

♦ **Feelings and emotions are present from birth.** While the neocortex, and therefore, rational and verbal thought, does not fully develop until around the age of 5 or 6, the amygdala is fully functional at birth, allowing infants to "tell" those in the environment, generally through tears or laughter, smiles or whines, what it needs to survive and thrive. It also means that the emotions we feel prior to the time the verbal brain is more fully developed may have no words to describe them. These feelings are still stored in the amygdala and can reappear when we are adults, making us feel anxious without being able to "explain" why in words.

♦ **Feelings are more potent than thoughts.** There are more neural connections from the amygdala to the neocortex than vice versa. The fact that there are more emotional messages going to the neocortex than there are rational thoughts traveling to the amygdala means that our feelings can overwhelm our thoughts as they do in panic attacks, for example. It is why strategies to contain painful emotions and keep them from surfacing are so difficult to maintain without constant vigilance.

♦ **Feelings convey far more complex messages than thoughts.**
The amygdala perceives complex patterns instantaneously.
Unlike the neocortex which operates in a more simple, linear
fashion, the emotional brain relies on whole patterns and first
impressions, reacting instantaneously to the most striking
aspects, and allowing us to respond immediately to potential
danger without having to stop and think. This feature provides
us a significant advantage when it comes to survival.

The amygdala plays a critical role in our well-being. It determines
how serene and intuitive we are, how well our instincts protect us,
how easily and how well we make critical decisions. It establishes
how connected we are to our inner voice, and how full of meaning
and sure of our direction we are. It is the source of our unique
sense of self, of what we like and
value. Whenever we have trouble
with instincts, intuition, decision-
making, emotions, the meaning or
direction of life, it is the amygdala
that is involved and where the
problem lies.

> My teacher said to me, 'The
> treasure house within you
> contains everything, and you
> are free to use it. You don't
> need to seek outside.'
> —*Zen Master Dazhu*

It is an unhealthy amygdala that is implicated whenever we
experience struggle, distress, emotional turmoil, whenever we have
persistent difficulty making decisions or confusion about what we
feel or the meaning or direction of our lives. Whenever we
behave in co-dependent or enabling ways, when we are
manipulated by others, when we choose dysfunctional
relationships, it is the amygdala not the rational part of the brain
that is in trouble, not the neocortex.

In fact, there is evidence that emotional trauma and the effort to
keep feelings suppressed affects the size of the amygdala.
Children who are anxious have a larger amygdala than those who
are not, whereas long term stress appear to actually shrinks the

amygdala and hippocampus (though, luckily, we may be able to reverse the shrinkage).

So, why, if the amygdala is stronger and faster than the neocortex, isn't it working more effectively in your life? To get to the answer to that question, we need to ask ourselves a deeper one. Why, in a country of such enormous wealth and resources, with great freedom and significant leisure time, with state-of-the-art medicine and mental health facilities, do millions of Americans suffer from emotional distress? And why is that number is growing?

From Turmoil to Tranquility

CHAPTER 2

♦ ♦ ♦ ♦ ♦

You Are Not Alone

An Emotional Infection of Epidemic Proportions

Take the first step in faith. You don't have to see the whole staircase, just take the first step. *Martin Luther King, Jr.*

66 Just tell me what's wrong with me." Debbie pleads desperately. An attractive woman in her early forties, Debbie suffers from chronic worry and obsessive thoughts, insomnia, severe anxiety mixed with periods of profound depression and occasional bursts of anger. She has painful episodes of fibromyalgia and is worried that she may be developing adult-onset diabetes, a disease that runs in her family.

"I've read books, attended seminars, listened to radio psychologists, talked to therapists. I think I understand my issues, but I don't *feel* any better. Sometimes, I think I must be either stupid or weak! People tell me to just 'get over it' and get on with my life. But no matter how hard I try, I just can't seem to do it. What's *wrong* with me?"

Debbie is not alone. Despite a culture of unprecedented wealth and unlimited resources, Americans are in a great deal of emotional and physical turmoil. According to the National Association for Mental Illness, more than 20 million of us will experience major depression or manic depression during our lifetime, and almost 30% of all Americans will suffer from a mental or substance abuse problem in any one year.[2] For the first time in history, stress-related and auto-immune disorders are the major cause of death and disease.

> 48% of all Americans between 15 and 54 will experience a psychological disorder during their lifetime!
> —*Practice Directorate*

Jon, Debbie's ex-husband, believes that her troubled childhood left her with permanent scars that no amount of therapy can erase. "It was not a healthy situation," he comments. "Her father was an alcoholic, and her mother was very controlling." At the same time, Jon knows that not *everybody* who had a painful childhood suffers from anxiety and depression. "Debbie's childhood, though not perfect by any means, was not as bad as many have had and been able to overcome," he adds.

Debbie's mother thinks her daughter isn't really trying. "I think she enjoys wallowing in pain. I think she gets something out of it," she offers. "I don't care what Debbie tells you, her childhood was pretty darn good. I'm convinced she is just tying to get attention."

But Debbie doesn't act like she enjoys the pain or wants the attention. She pursues every self-help fad that promises even a whisper of improvement. She has tried positive thinking, cognitive therapy, meditation, and medication. She has struggled with

---

[2] *In order to keep distractions to a minimum, sources for all statistics are found in the Resources section of the book.*

exercise, analysis, religion, and 12- step programs. For Debbie, the end result of years of therapy and mood-altering pills is more pain, not less. What was once mild anxiety sometimes now erupts into full-blown panic. What was once the blues is now clinical depression.

Dr. Williams believes Debbie has a chemical imbalance. "It's just physical," he tells her, and prescribes Xanax to relieve her symptoms when Prozac doesn't work. Debbie dislikes taking pills but feels desperate to get some relief. The medication helps a little, she thinks. The anxiety seems to be muted, but it isn't gone, and her life is just as chaotic as it always was.

Sarah, Debbie's friend, tells her to just forget about it and "get out of herself," thinking that the problem is mainly one of self-absorption. But while Debbie has tried to distract

> We are all ill: but even a universal sickness implies an idea of health.
> —*Lionel Trilling*

herself by working hard and doing good deeds, life crises continue to plague her, and the pain comes raging back when she least expects it.

The bottom line is that Debbie's family and friends have no idea how to help her. They can't figure out how such a wonderful person suffers from such low self-esteem and attracts so many dysfunctional relationships. In unguarded moments, they will tell you how tired they are of listening to her complaints. As for Debbie, she is exhausted with the effort, distrustful of therapists, and occasionally contemplates suicide.

An Epidemic of Distress

Does this sound like you or someone you love? If so, you are not alone. Unprecedented numbers of Americans are suffering from anxiety and depression.

Anxiety disorders *are the #1 mental health problem in the United States.*

The National Institute for Mental Health (NIMH) estimates these disorders affect 13% of all American adults and 13 million children between the ages of 9 and 17, including:

♦ 11.5 million phobics

♦ 4 million living with a constant state of anxiety

♦ 3.5 million enduring post-traumatic stress disorder

♦ 1.5 million suffering from panic attacks

♦ 2.5 million with OCD (obsessive compulsive disorder)

Depression, *often a byproduct of prolonged anxiety and stress, is quickly catching up.*

♦ One of the most exhaustive surveys found that in any given year, 9.5 percent of Americans – 25 million people – meet the diagnostic criteria for a mood disorder.

♦ 1 person kills themselves every 17 minutes

♦ 5 million Americans have tried to kill themselves

The Financial Cost

The financial drag on the economy and the resources spent trying to "feel better" and "get better" are enormous. More than $165 billion is spent on alcohol abuse alone. Another $44 billion is spent on depression, including medical costs, absenteeism, and reduced productivity, $42 billion is for doctor bills and workplace losses associated with anxiety disorders, and $5 billion goes for costs associated with gambling, including legal fees, court costs, jail expenses, lost wages, and bankruptcy.

For one Fortune 500 manufacturing company, insurance-covered mental health and substance abuse costs alone accounted for 30%

of the health expenditures for men aged 18 – 44. Heart disease was the second most expensive disorder.

Yet these epidemics continue unabated.

♦ There are more than 5 million pathological or problem gamblers in the U.S., and over 15 million more are at risk—those who have gambled at least once to relieve uncomfortable feelings.

♦ More than 11 million Americans are addicted to the Internet.

♦ Between 8 and 16 million Americans have a sexual addiction.

♦ The American murder rate is ten times that of other western nations

♦ Americans make up only 5% of the world's population but consume 50% of its cocaine.

And the physical consequences are growing. A full 75% of all visits to primary care physicians result from stress-related disorders.

Even more distressing, evidence suggests that despite all that we are spending in money, time and resources to get better, we may actually be getting worse. The World Health Organization (WHO)

> Predictions are that the future will bring an exponential increase in mental problems.
> —Gro Brundtland, M. D., Director General, WHO

estimates that by 2020, depression will be the second leading cause of "lost years of healthy life" worldwide—exceeded only by systemic heart disease.

And the rate is not slowing.

♦ A study by the WHO indicates that the odds of developing an anxiety disorder have doubled in the past 40 years.

♦ Depressive disorders are appearing earlier in life in people born in recent decades compared to the past.

- Four of the 10 leading causes of disability in the U.S. and other developed countries are mental disorders – major depression, bipolar disorder, schizophrenia, and obsessive-compulsive disorder.

Even adults in their 20s and 30s are experiencing angst. *Quarterlife Crisis* details the distress felt by the "20 Somethings," as a lack of meaning, direction, and spiritual ennui.

Our youngest children are suffering more too:

- The fastest growing gambling addiction rate is among high school and college teenagers—a rate two times that of adults.

- One in every eight teens is reported to be suffering from depression.

- More than one million children are taking Ritalin, a powerful stimulant, a rate that is five times higher than the rest of the world, and their numbers show no signs of abating.

- Suicide among children and teens has tripled in the past 40 years, despite the fact that Prozac, once the darling drug for depression (and a drug one million children take), now comes in peppermint flavor.

- At least 12% of youngsters under the age of 17 – 7.5 million – have a diagnosable mental illness.

In addition, cross-cultural studies show that the United States has one of the highest rates of emotional distress worldwide and hint that industrialized nations may be more prone to emotional distress than many of the less industrialized. Rates reported for depression are 12% for American men, 26% for American women, compared to a rate

Even more homogenized industrial cultures are not immune. Japan's combined murder and suicide rate is the same as the combined rate for the United States: 21 per every 100,000 residents.

of 2.5% for Iceland and 3.3% for India. In fact, our rate corresponds closely to the depression rate in Uganda – 14.3% for men and 22.6% for women.

Another WHO study of 30,000 people in seven countries measured the percentage of persons who had experienced at least one mental illness. The statistics were 48% for Americans compared to 40% for the Netherlands, 38% for Germany, 37% for Canada, 36% for Brazil, 20% for Mexico and just 12% for Turkey.

Something is seriously wrong.

CHAPTER 3

♦ ♦ ♦ ♦ ♦

Lookin' for Help
in All the Wrong Places
Chasing the Cures that Don't

Our problem is not ignorance, it's all the things we know that ain't so. *Will Rogers*

A recent client commented about his past experience with the psychiatric community:

After the first psychiatrist, I continued therapy with a new person, for an additional 2 ½ years, and right away this psychiatrist prescribed me Xanax. I did take very low dosage, but I felt I was doing all the talking. And even though this person seemed to be listening more effectively, I just felt I wasn't getting anywhere.

*But I kept going thinking that eventually he would tell me
or give me a magic word or key or something to say this is
the way you are thinking, and this is what you need to do.
And I didn't get this once. And at $85 a week, it didn't give
me anything back. All it did was give me lethargy. I just
felt tired most of the time. I started on Xanax pretty heavily
because I was just a wreck. I was a wreck. But I thought
he was going to give me the magic cure. Never happened.*

Trying to Get Well

In the eyes of many, those who suffer
from emotional distress are either too
stupid to "get it" or too weak to do what
they know they should do—get rid of
the bum, stop drinking, look for another
job, or speak up.

> We have more
> knowledge than our
> ancestors, but not
> more understanding.
> —Arnold Toynbee

Nothing could be further from the truth. People who are in turmoil
are all too aware of the effect their dysfunction has on their own
lives and the lives of those who love them. Emotional torment is a
great motivator: most people in emotional distress are creative and
persistent in their efforts to escape their agony. But they often
seem to be caught in a wicked circle, blindly chasing after the
latest bromide, working harder to control the pain but going
nowhere.

The Intellect Can't

"If I really understood my issues, I would feel better," states
Samantha, confidently. It is an American article of faith, the
foundation of psychiatrists' practices, personal improvement
seminars, radio-therapy programs, and makes self-help books the
blockbusters they are today.

I ask Samantha, if she understands her issues better than she did a
decade ago.

"Absolutely," she declares. The rest of the audience nods vigorously in agreement.

"And do you *feel* a lot better than you did before you acquired all that insight?" I ask, addressing the group at large. There are embarrassed smiles from a number of participants. They glance hesitantly at each other. "No," most of them reluctantly admit, they don't really *feel* much better. "Then what makes you think working harder on understanding your issues will help?" Invariably, the room erupts in nervous laughter.

> Committed as therapists are to talking about various issues, there is no evidence to indicate that these dialogues help their clients.
> —*Terence Campbell*

Samantha has lots of company. Psychiatry is the fifth most visited medical specialty, with almost 20 million visits a year to those in private practice alone; hundreds of millions make annual visits to family doctors because of emotional distress; far more self-help books are bought than any other genre.

The results from meta-analyses of thousands of studies is unmistakable. The hard evidence is that, with few scattered exceptions (which will be addressed in later chapters), no one therapy seems to be more effective than any other; small rather than large changes in behavior and feelings are the rule; and most changes are short-lived.

Nor does the training of the therapist seem to matter. Clients are no more likely to improve with highly-trained psychiatrists than they are with untrained nonprofessionals. Psychiatrists, psychologists, social workers all appear to be equally effective or ineffective, and ability does not improve with experience. In one study, patients were randomly

> Most studies report that 50% to 80% of suicide victims had seen a physician or health care professional within 1 to 3 months prior to the suicide.
> —*Psychiatric News*

assigned to two different groups – one received therapy from professional psychologists, the other from university professors with no psychological background at all. The groups responded equally well.

Physician Heal Thyself

Even therapists, more knowledgeable than the public at large about the intricacies of the human mind are no better adjusted. Though professional counselors have received far more therapy than any other group, there is no evidence those of any type do better, feel better, or overcome their problems better than anyone else. One survey of medical professionals found that psychiatrists suffered from *more* marital and sexual problems than any other group. Their suicide rate is *one of the highest* of any in the medical profession, and their drug and alcohol abuse is rampant. Even the best and the brightest therapists do no better than the average American.

> Any man who goes to a psychiatrist ought to have his head examined.
> —Samuel Goldwyn

• Sigmund Freud suffered from agoraphobia his entire life. He dreaded traveling by train because of the potential for an accident, avoided ceremonies of any kind, and suffered from frequent anxiety and attacks of hysteria. He was tyrannical, impatient, and caustic. In a series of letters to his fiancée Martha, Freud, though he knew his jealousy of Fritz Wahle, her music teacher, was unreasonable, attempts to understand his feelings and resolve them. He fails miserably and erupts in intense rage. "When the memory of your letter to Fritz comes back to me," he writes, "I lose all control of myself, and had I the power to destroy the whole world, I would do so without hesitation."

• "Aaron Green," a psychiatrist who underwent 15 years of psychoanalysis, said, "As I grew less nasty and pugnacious and argumentative—as I began more and more to say to myself, 'Hell, you don't have to do that anymore'—I grew more and more anxious about things that I had never been anxious about before. Like being in crowds and sitting in the balcony at the theatre. I also developed a speaking anxiety, which I still have, and which really troubles me."

• Renowned therapist and author David Viscott could zero in on a patient's problem in less than 30 seconds but could not eliminate his own demons. At the time of his death, he was depressed, involved in a tempestuous, addictive relationship with his second wife, estranged from his daughter and other friends, and on the financial skids. "Talk Radio's Shrink Was Tough on People Who Came to Him for Help. But Many Swore by His Advice," reads a headline from *Los Angeles Magazine*. "Too Bad He Didn't Call Himself for the Same Counseling."

Each of these exceptionally intelligent, moral, well-meaning individuals had intimate knowledge of their problems. They spent their lives thinking, talking,

> Theorizing is a way to avoid the pain.
> —*Tom Stone*

writing about, dissecting, pondering, and examining their childhoods and neuroses. Despite the time spent and singular lack of progress, each of them clung to the belief that thinking about their issues would eventually give them inner peace. Nothing could shake them from the firm—and mistaken—conviction that they could achieve serenity if they could just "figure it out."

One of the problems with this approach is that the left brain – the part of the brain that is trying to "figure it out," is notoriously inaccurate. Split brain studies have shown that while the right brain is accurate in its perception of facts, the left brain is not. The left brain tries to weave a story that ties the pieces together in a comprehensive way that makes sense. The left brain cares not a

> Our greatest battles are that with our own minds.
> —*Jameson Frank*

whit if what makes sense is true or not.

The fact is, anxiety, fear, depression, and anger cannot be "cured" by the intellect. Anyone who has experienced obsessive thoughts or has been caught in the throes of analysis paralysis knows in their gut that expecting to change feelings by thinking about them is about as effective as expecting to pass a geology exam by playing Beethoven's Fifth. It just isn't going to happen.

Willpower Won't

So if brainpower does not solve psychological problems, how about willpower – positive thinking, keeping busy or distracting yourself?

"Sometimes, when I am nervous or depressed, I'll go to a movie, rent an engrossing video, or go to a party," comments Angela. "Other times I read positive thinking books or do affirmations. But usually, I just take on an extra project at work. My boss loves me because I am always willing to work overtime. It keeps my mind completely occupied and I don't have time to think about anything that is bothering me. It really helps."

> An expert is someone who knows more and more about less and less, until eventually he knows everything about nothing.
> —Anonomyous

"And what happens when the project is finished, the movie is over, or the party ends?" I ask.

"Well, usually the uncomfortable feelings come back, so I just keep up the effort."

"In other words, it often just puts off the inevitable," I offer. The group titters in recognition.

Unable to eliminate anxiety and depression by "figuring out" their problems, most people turn to behaviors that will distract them. They vow to keep busy, "forget about it," and bury themselves in other activities. "After all, my painful childhood happened a long time ago," they reason. "There is nothing I can do about it now

except forget about it, get on with life, and make it the best I can."
Like Scarlet O'Hara, they will think about it tomorrow.

But does this strategy work? Can developing a strong will
consistently produce peacefulness? The lives of those who are
famous for their courage provide some clues.

- General George S. Patton, one of the toughest warriors in
America with a will that was legendary, was nevertheless
unable to conquer his own impulsiveness. Though well
aware of how much his behavior hurt his military career, he
was unable to control his temper, bursting into frequent
rages, slapping two soldiers in evacuation hospitals and
calling them cowards. His frequent outbursts continued to
his death.

- Billed as "The Little Boy Who Can't Be Damaged,"
Buster Keaton was tossed about by his father—once
incurring a head wound that knocked him out for 18
hours—to the delight of vaudeville audiences and the
consternation of the Society for the Prevention of Cruelty
to Children. Stoically enduring concussions, sprains, and
broken bones, he soon developed the characteristic stone
face that became his trademark. As an adult, though
insisting his father had not
emotionally damaged him,
Keaton drank excessively,
had trouble with
relationships, and developed
an obsession for practical
jokes that made others
suffer.

> In Victorian times,
> willpower was everything:
> you could be the captain
> of your soul, the master
> of your fate if only you
> tried hard enough.
> —Bernie Zilbergeld

- Laura Schlessinger, once this country's most popular
radio personality, exhorts her listeners to forget their
feelings and use their willpower to "do what's right."
Although she is not a shrink and has never undergone

therapy, she is a licensed marriage, family, and child counselor and has insight into her own emotional baggage. Has her knowledge or strength of character made her a tranquil person? Hardly. Despite the 50-plus pages devoted to honoring one's mother and father in one of her latest books, Dr. Laura has no relationship with either her mother or younger sister and once told a reporter she was an only child. She bubbles with anger and often impatiently cuts off callers before they have a chance to state their issues. She is a national scold, a defensive bundle of nerves, unable to hear differing opinions without taking them personally.

The message is clear. Strength of character is not the panacea for the serenity we seek. Though immensely useful for stints as a prisoner of war, surviving in the desert, enduring an abusive childhood, or controlling behavior, willpower is not an effective strategy for eliminating emotional pain.

And Pills Don't

Since intellectual effort and force of will don't ease emotional distress significantly or permanently, perhaps it is caused by a chemical imbalance. Perhaps only medication can produce lasting serenity.

This is a trendy idea. Americans fill more than 40 million mood disorder prescriptions annually and more than 103 new psychoactive drugs are currently being tested including 26 for depression. Medication was prescribed in more than 70% of 1994 visits to psychiatrists, up from 53% a decade earlier, and the number is growing exponentially at all age levels—even for children and preschoolers. More than a half-million children now take anti-depressants, and the pediatric market is one

> A review of the literature found no clinical proof that antidepressants are effective in children.
> *Rhoda and Seymour Fisher (both PhD's)*

of the fastest growing, increasing ten-fold in the last four years, even though all studies to date indicate that these drugs are no more effective with children than placebos.

Unfortunately, as we will see, many psychotropic medications prescribed to "correct a chemical imbalance" actually do the opposite. Not only do they actually decrease the amount of the neurotransmitter that is made naturally by the body, but the time it takes for the brain to rebound after the drug is discontinued, can have devastating psychological effects. There is, in addition, evidence that these drugs may work by damaging the connections between brain neurons and even by destroying receptor sites. Whether or not this damage is temporary or long lasting has not yet been determined.

Clinical Psychiatric News recently stated that "despite decades of progress in developing psychiatric medications, there has been little change in the rate of suicide in the last quarter century." Even the makers of most psychotropic medicines admit that their medications merely help with symptoms but cannot be considered a cure.

Mark volunteers that he has been diagnosed with a chemical imbalance and has tried psychotropic medications. "Did medication eliminate your pain?" I ask. "No," he answers, "I tried a number of them. They dulled the pain, but it didn't go away completely."

> If at first you don't succeed, try again. Then quit. No use being a damn fool about it.
> —W. C. Fields

"And is your life running smoothly right now?" I ask. "Have your life crises disappeared?"

"Well, not exactly," he admits. I can see nods of agreement from other parts of the room.

"Then why do you have the idea that medication is any more effective than alcohol, marijuana, food, or anything else you might take to distract yourself from the turmoil?"

Those who have tried medication—legal or illegal—recognize the conundrum. The dirty little secret of pharmaceutical companies is that psychotropic medications don't cure emotional distress. At best, they dull it, providing a kind of "chemical lobotomy" by suppressing uncomfortable feelings rather than eliminating them, rather like taking a pain killer and expecting a tumor to go away.

Dr. Peter Breggin, M.D., co-author of *Your Drug May Be Your Problem: How and Why to Stop Taking Psychiatric Medications,* states,

> *Psychiatry bases its argument for biological causes of mental disorder on the grounds that drugs work. But there is no necessary connection between the relief a drug provides and the underlying cause of the distress. People use alcohol, marijuana, and a variety of other substances including food to reduce emotional suffering. This says almost nothing about the source of that suffering. It is no different with psychiatric medications.*

Certainly, if psychotropic medicines were "curative" we would not expect the sometimes tragic behavior of those who are taking them:

• According to the autopsy, student Eric Harris was under the influence of the psychiatric drug Luvox at the time of the Columbine High School murder spree.

• Brynn Hartman was taking Zoloft at the time she murdered

> Scientists have shown that Ritalin appears to cause changes in brain function similar to those that occur with amphetamines and cocaine that remain after the therapeutic effects have dissipated.
> —*University of Buffalo*

her husband, comedian Phil Hartman, and then turned the gun on herself.

Not only is the efficacy of these medications in doubt, there is also significant dispute as to whether or not the idea of a "chemical imbalance" actually exists. Results of experiments with serotonin, believed by some to be an indicator of feelings of well-being, are mixed at best and can often be corrected by increasing exercise, getting more sunlight, changing one's diet, or even using over-the-counter substances such as 5HTP, a health-food supplement.

Dr. Breggin continues,

> *Of course serotonin is involved in the obsessive-compulsive process. It's involved in every mental and emotional process. . . [but] there are . . . no known biochemical abnormalities in the brains of people routinely seen by psychiatrists, including those with the most severe labels, such as schizophrenia, major depression, or manic-depressive (bipolar) disorder.*

At best, doctors seem to be guessing as to the biological cause of emotional distress. Worse, they are prescribing medication that is powerful, unpredictable, possibly addictive, and in many cases, ineffective.

The Placebo Effect.

Often, the "improvement" reported after either psychotherapy or medication can be attributed the "placebo effect," A well-known phenomenon in medicine, it is

> The hardest part about gaining any new idea is sweeping out the false idea occupying that niche. As long as that niche is occupied, evidence and proof and logical demonstration get nowhere.
> —*Robert Heinlein*

perhaps even more prevalent in the field of psychology. Many studies have documented that placebo agents – pills, "fake therapy" etc. – have an effectiveness rate of anywhere from 30% to

70%. Irving Kirsch, scientist and author of *The Emperor's New Drugs* claims that most of our favorite psychotropic drugs – Prozac, Zoloft and Paxil, for example – "may have no meaningful pharmacological effect at all."

In one of the more arresting studies, fourteen depressed patients were prescribed placebo pills for a week and *told that the pills were inert*. All fourteen responded positively to the treatment. In follow-up interviews, six believed the pills actually contained medication, four said it was the most effective medicine they had ever taken and 5 wanted to continue taking it. In addition,

♦ Many double-blind placebo studies – those in which neither the therapist nor the patient supposedly know if they are receiving active medication or a sugar pill – are invalid. Because the active medication generally produces side-effects and the placebos do not, patients and their doctors are often able to accurately guess which they have been receiving.

♦ In a study of patients suffering from panic disorder, one group received 12 sessions of cognitive behavioral therapy, the other a placebo therapy, one in which the therapist listened sympathetically but made no specific suggestions. Both groups did equally well.

♦ When a placebo with side-effects is used in an antidepressant study, the difference between the placebo and the antidepressant is virtually washed out.

> Pain and fear are necessary components to life; suffering and worry are unnecessary and destructive.
> —*Gavin DeBecker*

And finally, one study showed that a significant amount of psychological improvement often occurs *between the time the patient makes the first appointment and when they arrive for it*. In other words, the improvement is based on the internal *decision* the patient makes to address the problem, *not* on the therapy itself.

Angst and the Human Condition

Is serenity a mirage, as many philosophers think? Is pain just a natural part of life? Some, perhaps, but not as much as we seem to suffer.

Helen has battled anxiety for decades. In frustration, she pours out her heart to her husband Nate. "I feel like I am in a tunnel, crawling up a steep hill," she moans. "I can see the light at the end of the tunnel, but no matter how hard I try, I never get any closer. I am so tired, so exhausted from the effort. I know the light is there, a place where I can be free of pain, I can see it, but I don't know how to reach it."

"There is no such place," Nate offers quietly. "Everybody suffers. It's just part of the human condition. The only thing you can do to feel better is to drop the idea that it should be any better. In other words, 'get over it.'"

Is Nate right?

Thankfully, he is not. There is something beyond therapy, willpower and pills. Something far better than suffering.

It is an innate emotional healing system with the power to erase the pain of the past and to virtually eliminate future life crises.

It is fast, free, effective, and efficient. It requires no therapy, experts, group discussion, or medication.

It is a gift from Mother Nature that we were born with. And no matter how much damage we do to it, we cannot completely eradicate it.

It is also the best kept secret in America.

CHAPTER 4

◆ ◆ ◆ ◆ ◆

Mother Nature's Miracle Medicine:

The Mind as a Self-Correcting Organism

In the Hippocratic view, disease was a disharmony of conflicting humors and elements, and systems were the organism's attempt to establish a new harmony. *Elio Frattaroli*

That secret is homeostasis, Mother Nature's gift to all organisms. It is the tendency of all living things to return to a state of health and well being, all by themselves, *if we let them*.

Forests begin to flourish within days after a devastating fire, the body bounces back after a bout with the flu and new research provides tantalizing hints that **our psyche too – especially the amygdala or emotional brain – is specifically designed to self-**

correct, dissolve old emotional memories and return us to a state of serenity. In fact, we know that the emotional brain even works hard during our dreams to process and dissolve the emotional damage it has endured during the day.

Homeostasis is an amazingly complex process that operates without our direct control but needs our cooperation. The key to emotional, physical and even social, political and economic health is to understand how emotional homeostasis works and *better cooperate with it* so it can do its job.

So why don't most of us, and even most doctors seem to know about this process? Lets take a short 30-minute detour, get a grasp on the 500-year old "Cartesian-Newtonian paradigm," how it led to the medical model of mental illness and why reality itself is not as we have been taught.

Rene Descartes and the Medical Model

Before the 1600s, the time of famed philosopher Rene Decartes, the father of modern medicine, the mind and body were considered as one. Interested in obtaining human bodies for scientific research, but blocked by the Church's jurisdiction over the soul, Descartes declared the mind and body to be separate entities and claimed the realm of the physical as his own. The Pope agreed, and from that moment on, both modern medicine and science itself have been based on a mythical split between mind and body, material and spiritual, particle and wave.

When ideas go unexamined and unchallenged for a long time, certain things happen. They become mythological, and they become very, very powerful.
—E. L. Doctorow

At roughly the same time, Sir Isaac Newton proposed that the universe was ruled by certain mechanical laws: plot all the planets in the solar system at any one point in time, and one could plot them accurately for eternity, he thought. Newtonians believed that the result of rigorous rational, scientific study would and should be the ability to predict and control nature.

This must have been great news for people who lived in the agricultural age, who were victims of floods and earthquakes, disease and pestilence, and could rely only on the mercy of the gods to which they prayed. Surely they grasped these ideas with great enthusiasm.

But the brain, mind, body and even the universe, for that matter, are neither mechanical in nature nor are they separate entities. As quantum physicists have since discovered, all of these are complex, interrelated, living *systems*. Like all systems, they continuously interact with their environment and develop new characteristics as part of the evolutionary process.

> Descartes inadvertently reinforced a tendency to avoid the unsettling awareness of inner conflict by divorcing our mental life from our experience of the body.
> —Elio Frattaroli

In such a world, where change is the only constant, where all the parts have "will," complete control is impossible. Though we can influence these systems, no matter how advanced our technology becomes, in the end, they are ruled by Mother Nature, whose will is always more powerful in the long run than our own. Though we may believe that we are the wisest beings in the universe, it is only an illusion. Nature bases its own decisions on what is best for the survival, health and joy of *all life in the long run*. More effective than trying to control her is to learn all we can about these systems and cooperate with them.

Systems are Connected and Wholistic

Because Newtonian-Cartesian science and modern medicine are based on a separatist model they focus primarily on individual parts – organs, cells, brain chemicals, and germs, for example. This is fine as far as it goes, but it is similar to expecting a listener to have an accurate appreciation for a brownie by describing flour, sugar, butter, baking soda, eggs, and chocolate. A truer picture of reality requires that we also look at the whole, at how these parts organize themselves, how they interconnect and make decisions, and how they struggle to maintain their own balance and integrity against human behavior that tries to control them.

♦ The Medical Model has proposed that depression, for example is caused by a shortage of the neurotransmitter serotonin. Doctors prescribe Prozac or similar medications to correct what is viewed as a "chemical imbalance," but ignore potential lifestyle causes of serotonin shortage – lack of sunshine in some locales, too little exercise, or too many refined carbohydrates in the diet, for example.

♦ For decades, farmers have fed their cattle and poultry the female hormone estrogen to make them fat and thus more profitable. Recently, however, scientists have begun to draw connections between the decrease in male fertility, the early onset of puberty in girls, and the increase of estrogens in water contaminated by animal waste.

♦ Though the development of antibiotics has been of great benefit to mankind, too many doctors downplay the devastating effects these medications can have on the immune system. Children who are given antibiotics to cure respiratory and ear infections have *more* relapses than children that are not so medicated. Antibiotics kill not only the bad germs but the good germs as well, and it is a rare doctor who will prescribe probiotics to replenish the supply of good bacteria to the patient on antibiotics.

> There is only one nature – the division into science and engineering is a human imposition, not a natural one. Indeed, the division is a human failure; it reflects our limited capacity to comprehend the whole.
> —*Bill Wulf*

Systems Are Multiple and Overlapping

It is not just the brain and its neurons that create our minds. The psyche is made up of multiple interlocking systems. Neuroscientist Candace Pert in her book *Molecules of Emotion* documents the extraordinary connections between three different systems – the brain, our hormones and the immune system and

> *shows how the molecules of emotion run every system in our body and how this communication system is in effect a demonstration of the bodymind's intelligence, an intelligence wise enough to seek wellness and one that can potentially keep us healthy and disease-free without the modern high-tech medical intervention we now rely on.*

Her research demonstrates that emotions are inseparable from our physiology, that the psyche exists throughout the body, and she establishes the bio-molecular basis for phenomenon such as "gut reaction," and the connection between emotional well-being and physical health.

Systems Are Intelligent and Alive

Even the lowly bacteria make decisions. Recent research from the University of Wisconsin-Madison reveals that germs are equipped with receptors on their surface that allow them to talk to one another, learn from their surroundings, act in concert, and

> I believe in God, only I spell it Nature.
> —*Frank Lloyd Wright*

decide which way to move – from a dangerous environment to a desirable one, for example.

Unfortunately, medicine in general and psychiatry in particular have not caught on to this concept of aliveness. Doctors continue to treat the body as if it were the engine of a car – as if one could change one part of the entity without affecting any other.

♦ While the idea behind Selective Serotonin Re-uptake Inhibitors SSRI's is to *increase* the amount of the neurotransmitter serotonin in the system, *it actually does the opposite*. Locking serotonin into its receptor for longer than nature intends produces a cascade effect. The body does not sit idly by. Being alive, intelligent and interconnected, it quickly catches on to this ruse and *decreases* the amount of serotonin it manufactures. As patients increase their Prozac dosage to get the same effect, the body further decreases its serotonin production. As a result, 34% of all patients experience the dreaded "Prozac Poop-out," a condition in which the body is producing so little serotonin, that no amount of the drug will work. Other side-effects include persistent sexual problems, experienced by a whopping 60% of patients, and serious withdrawal symptoms suffered by 50%.

In addition, these medications, though advertised as *selective* serotonin uptake inhibitors, are nothing of the kind. Only 5% of all the serotonin in the body is found in the brain. The rest is distributed throughout the rest of the body, much of it in the intestinal tract where it regulates rhythmic movements, kneading food through the stomach; and in blood vessels where it helps to control the flow of blood and plays an important role in clotting. Serotonin also controls a host of hormones that

> We still do not know one-thousandth of one percent of what nature has revealed to us.
> —*Albert Einstein*

regulate a multitude of other physiological responses such as the flexing process in the gut. SSRIs affect *all* the serotonin receptors, not just the ones in the brain!

♦ Our immune system is not mechanical. It has memory and is able to learn. In one novel study of cancer patients, scientists drew blood just before and after patients entered the same hospital where they had previously received chemotherapy. Blood counts showed a decrease of white blood cells *even before the scheduled treatment was administered.* The immune system, it seems, had learned to decrease production of white blood cells – in anticipation of chemotherapy!

◆ Our hormones also appear to operate in the service of a greater good. Men living with women experience a drop in testosterone immediately after their partners give birth. Their testosterone level recovers approximately three weeks after the birth. Interestingly, testosterone levels for those men living with children in the home remains lower than those living without children. Nature, it seems, wants intact families, with fathers staying close at hand.

Systems Are Purposeful

Though systems may sometimes seem arbitrary, they are usually not. They are instead designed to keep each of their parts alive and healthy by providing a constant stream of information about both the external and internal worlds. These messages contain critical

information that allows us to perceive danger, navigate in unfamiliar territory, intuitively know when we are being deceived, and sense when we are getting sick. Whether or not each of the parts stays healthy depends on how much attention and respect we give to these messages.

> We need humility to know that truth can be ephemeral, that this can be but one version of the truth.
> —Ken Auletta

New brain technology that takes moving pictures of the brain in action reveals that:

◆ The body, through its senses receives messages from the external environment and automatically prioritizes them according to how important they are to our survival. In one study, subjects who were presented with pictures of forests and fields saw spiders and snakes faster than they did trees and flowers.

◆ Chemical/electrical messages that are received compete with one another for attention and at the same time appear to "discuss" which should be passed on to the next neuron. This is a task of monumental proportions. There are billions of neurons, and trillions of connections from one neuron to another. A typical neuron can have millions of receptors on its surface, and up to 20,000 messages course along a single neural pathway at any one moment. One author likened the process to caucuses at political conventions in which each message tries to get other messages to cooperate and get on board so that their message is the one that will be passed on.

This work is done *for* us, without our conscious participation. If we are tired, the instructions are to sleep (not to gulp another three cups of coffee!). If we are hungry within an hour of eating, our body is telling us we might want to try something different at the next meal, perhaps more protein or less sugar. If we catch recurring infections, the message may be to examine our lifestyle and look at changing it.

Messages with emotional content are no different. Though the so-called medical establishment labels them "diseases," anxiety and depression are *physical* symptoms, information from the system asking us to pay attention to the fact that something is wrong and needs to be changed. If our children are insolent and unhappy, we are being told to probe deeper. If minor violence erupts in a faraway nation, it is a message to find out why and if necessary take corrective action before it develops into a major conflagration.

Systems Require Diversity

If you have ever asked yourself if you are *normal*, ask yourself the following. What is a "normal" cell in the body? Is it a brain cell? A liver cell? A skin cell? *All* the parts of the body are essential for it to work

> Everybody can be great . . because anybody can serve. You don't have to have a college degree to serve. You don't have to make your subject and verb agree to serve. You only need a heart full of grace, a soul generated by love.
>
> —*Martin Luther King, Jr.*

properly. No one part is more important than any other part. In a system, there is no such thing as normal. A cell may be healthy or not, this is a different matter. But normal, it is not.

If you think you should be "more like" someone else, that you should live up to some external idea, ask yourself what life would look like if we were all the same. The fact is, *nature not only prefers diversity, she requires it.*
This is not a "one-size-fits-all" universe. Some of us do best on high carbohydrate diets, some on protein. One is not "better" than

> Every blade of grass has its angel that bends over it and whispers grow, grow!
> —*The Talmud*

the other. But differences in our preferences will ensure that our species survives if certain food supplies are wiped out. Men have more immediate upper body strength, women more long-term strength for the same reason. One is not superior to the other. Both are important for survival. We are different. We are supposed to be different.

- Patients suffering from identical forms of brain damage often exhibit completely different symptoms

- Temperament appears to have genetic components. Babies can be identified as easy, slow to warm up and difficult from birth

- Males tend to encourage their children to be brave; females to be more comforting and protective. Both are needed for health and survival.

Each of us is part of a larger system. We are not all meant to be rocket scientists, linguistically brilliant, or musically talented. Despite

> You don't get harmony when everybody sings the same note.
> —*Doug Floyd*

advertisements that exhort us to take Paxil for social anxiety, we are not all created to be extroverts, social butterflies, skinny models, or even parents. If we were all the same, society would fall apart. Like pieces of a puzzle, we – our minds, our bodies, our families, our society – comprise a system, each unique part equally required for the system to work properly. Diversity ensures that whatever the environmental conditions, whatever disease or disaster might envelop the world, *some of us* will survive to pass on our genes.

Systems are Self-Correcting

One of the most remarkable characteristics of organic systems is their ability to recover from massive assaults. All organic systems have a built-in, self-correcting mechanism. Rivers, clogged with industrial pollutants run clean a decade later. The DOW-Jones, soaring above 10,000 returns to normal (to the disappointment of all). The body grows more immune-enhancing bacteria after antibiotics nearly eliminate them. And the brain eventually recovers its ability to make the requisite amounts of the neurotransmitter GABA (a neurotransmitter) even after years on Xanax.

> History is a vast early warning system.
> —Norman Cousins

If the damage is extensive, the system may need our help – massive clean-up activities, doses of probiotics, lengthy periods of time to "detox" from drugs, etc. But generally all the system needs to recover is our cooperation. *We have to let it.*

In order to do that, we need to fully appreciate the *value* of symptoms. **Our distress is *not* the problem. It is information *about* the problem,** important information which if attended to, understood and followed will bring us peace.

Control and the Law of Unintended Consequences

Unfortunately, however, what we usually do is push our uncomfortable feelings aside and derail Mother Nature's attempt to heal us. *Chronic* problems, be they physical, emotional, or social are a dead giveaway: something is stopping the self-correcting mechanism dead in its tracks! Generally, that something is treating the symptoms as if they were the disease and actively working against them. This works about as well as disconnecting the warning system of a car instead of taking it in for a complete check and service. Though no longer being annoyed by that pesky alarm, without attention, the car will eventually fall apart.

♦ We dose ourselves with aspirin to lower a fever. But the fever is intended to kill the bad bacteria; lowering or eliminating it can prolong disease.

♦ We take antibiotics to kill a particular germ and end up with an impaired immune system that is less able to fight the next invader, and with powerful super-bacteria that have learned how to outwit the antibiotics we just took.

♦ We "make nice" with our spouse – pretending to agree just to keep the peace, grow apart and end up in divorce court.

♦ We take Xanax to cure anxiety, Prozac to eliminate depression, and often end up with greater life crises and less ability to deal naturally with our issues

The Dominator Model

The truth is, these systems are both elegant and extremely complex – far too intricate and interwoven to control. But attempts to dominate them are exactly what Newtonian-Cartesian thought and the medical models promote.

One of the most egregious examples I have ever encountered came from Scandinavia. Experimenters had succeeded in breaking the connection between stress and physical illness by

> Pray, n:. To ask that the laws of the universe be annulled in behalf of a single petitioner confessedly unworthy.
> —*Ambrose Bierce*

killing a few neurons in the brain. There was no acknowledgment that there might be good reasons why we get sick when we are stressed, that illness itself might be a message to back down and rest, or that the long term health of our entire system might depend on following this message.

The work was based on the idea that nature is wrong, that we need not pay attention to how we were constructed, and that we can substitute our intelligence for the genius of Mother Nature without consequence. We should be rational, "normal," and in control.

This is typical of almost all the advice that those who suffer receive from most in the medical establishment:

♦ Feelings are the problem and should be brought under the dominance of rational thought. Extensive schools of psychology and therapy are based on this erroneous notion.

♦ Most disease is an inevitable consequence of nature's errors rather than the result of poor lifestyle choices and failure to respond when the symptoms are the least severe.

♦ Life is difficult and there is no such thing as objective emotional health. The psychiatric bible, the Statistical and Diagnostic Manual lists mental diseases in terms of norms – how one compares with *others*, not in terms of how joyful or serene one is, how one's health compares with good health. (Given that 48% of Americans will suffer from a severe mental disorder at some time in their lives, these norms are problematic!)

It is time to put the dominator model to rest. While it has in some respects served us well, in others it has been counter-productive.

The Cooperator Model

Albert Einstein once defined insanity as doing the same thing over and over again, expecting different results. This is clearly what we have been doing for the last several decades. It is time for a radical change, time for a more wholistic model of mental health, one that focuses on how to cooperate with nature's systems, how to strengthen the self-correcting process

> Mitakuye Oyasin.
> [We are all related.]
> —Lakota Belief

instead of trying to decapitate it.

It is time to find out what our feelings are for, what nature intends when we are anxious or depressed, if shortages of neurotransmitters (if indeed there are such shortages) are purposeful, and what kind of lifestyle changes will help us live more joyful and tranquil lives.

The system is your friend. It is intelligent, alive, reliable, faithful, and has your best interests in mind. It is far more intelligent than we, far more prescient, far wiser.

We must understand how nature does her job and let her. We must understand her process and rules and cooperate with them. We must first trust her genius and intelligence. And we can start by learning the language of Mother Nature, the language of emotions, feelings, and sensations.

> Nature, to be commanded,
> must be obeyed.
> —*Francis Bacon*

PART II
The Principles

Emotions as a
Second Language

The Language of Mother Nature

PART II
Russia

The Secret's In the Sensations

"Old Stuff"

Repression

The Positive Purpose of Pain

Addictions

Life Crises

Russia

◆ ◆ ◆ ◆ ◆

I awoke that morning already anxious, although I wasn't sure why. It was late October 1990. I had arrived just a few days previously and was staying in an old flat in a crumbling complex somewhere—I had no idea where—on the outskirts of Moscow. The days were gray, and the nights made grayer by the fact that my friend and lover had become suddenly and violently ill with some undiagnosed disease and had left to be nursed by his medically trained mother to save me from a similar fate. I would be in Russia for only a month, little time for us to be together, and neither of us had any idea of how long this unwelcome interruption would last. In the meantime, as the precious days ticked by, I spent my mornings alone with my thoughts and my afternoons and evenings at museums and plays, restaurants and art galleries, escorted by Volodia's friends and business acquaintances who were nice enough, but, by and large, did not speak much, if any, English.

I had met Volodia in the States a few months earlier, and we had fallen in love. One of Russia's first capitalists, Volodia commanded rooms and people—especially me—like the leader and aristocrat he was. His personal power and strength were thrilling and seductive. He had been back in Russia for almost three months, but there was so much chemistry that the 10,000 miles between Moscow and Los Angeles did not deter us.

He would take care of everything, he tenderly assured me just before I left the United States to spend a month with him in Russia. He would make all the arrangements for my stay, for travel, for entertainment. I wouldn't need any money. He had plenty. He *wanted* to take care of me. I hesitated. It was not my habit to rely on anyone else, but I was working hard on trusting people and his offer was serendipitous. With courage in hand and a lump in my throat, I took a deep breath. "Thank you." I murmured quietly. And in that moment, in more ways than I could have imagined, like a child, I put myself completely in his hands.

Now, as I slowly awakened, on the third day of his illness, my mind raced nowhere in particular but darted back and forth and in circles, uncontrollably, despite my efforts to direct it in productive ways to this concern or that. It was 7 a.m. The bed was narrow and strange and lumpy, and I had planned to spend the day with an American friend in central Moscow. Tom was expected to call that morning around 9 to make arrangements for us to meet.

I arose and began the cumbersome process of preparing coffee, showering, and getting dressed. All the activities that were automatic at home took twice as long and required three times as much thought here. The thinking involved in this morning ritual was a welcome diversion from other more intrusive and disturbing thoughts.

I wonder how Volodia is feeling. Is he going to die? Pour milk into a metal carafe and find the coffee.

*Does he love me? Does he **really** love me?* Pour the coffee into the cup.

Maybe he really isn't sick. Maybe he doesn't love me. Pick out something to wear.

Maybe he's just being polite. What if he just didn't know how to tell me he wants me to leave. Shower, get dressed, and dry my hair. I try to force my mind to think about the office. What time is it in California, anyway? Can I call my assistant, or is it too late? Oh, too late. Maybe I could get some work done—does this flat have pencils and paper? Opening drawers, cupboards. There must be paper and pencils somewhere. Maybe TV. Perhaps CNN is on here.

Why hasn't he called? Plug in the TV, turn it on. Flip through the channels. Nothing in English. Flip through the channels again. Somewhere in the building a door slams shut. I hear the footsteps descending the stairs, past my door. I am silent. I know I am not supposed to be here. There is still a good deal of suspicion of foreigners—especially those staying in private flats. I don't want to get Volodia in trouble.

Does Volodia really love me, or is he faking his illness just to avoid me? Is he upset, or angry, or just inconvenienced, sorry that I was there, and wanting me to go home?

The fearful, strange thoughts came tumbling out, one after the other with increasing frequency and intensity. I didn't know which ones were real and which were not. I tried unsuccessfully to stop them. My body tensed, a lump formed in my throat, first the size of a marble, then a ping-pong ball, and then a tennis ball. I swallowed repeatedly in a vain attempt to push it away. Every cell, ragged and on edge, vibrated with anxiety. My body felt like a tuning fork. I began to pace faster and faster, hoping that continual motion would still the constant thoughts. It did not. I was terrified. Of what, I was not sure.

Why doesn't Tom call? I've got to get out of here. Every nerve was on edge. My heart raced and pounded. I could feel every sharp jagged edge of my life. I tried again to distract myself. Maybe a book. I looked for something—anything in English.

Maybe a deck of cards—solitaire? Could I make myself a deck of cards?

Why was this happening to me? How can I stop it? How can I escape this madness? Not everyone lives this way. Anxiety, dread, fear overwhelmed me. I was falling, floating, without boundaries, lightheaded, unconnected with reality. I was no longer sure of anything. Except that I was completely terrified. I picked up the phone. It was dead. The terror doubled.

I am here all alone. Perhaps I will die here alone. No one can call. Will anyone be able to tell if the phone is out of order? Will they know I'm in trouble, that I'm all alone? I hear other strange voices in the hall.

I considered the possibility of safely making it to the center of Moscow—surely there would be banks and hotels there where I could get my American money exchanged and call someone. *How would I get downtown?* I had a map of the Metro, but I didn't know where the closest station was. *What would I do if I got lost? I didn't even know my address.*

My body trembled with fear. An hour or two went by. It was early afternoon and I was running out of time. It was October and it would be dark by 5 p.m.

I must act now. I was driven by staggering fear. *I must find a Metro and get downtown. I must get help.*

Barely holding myself together, I threw on my coat, scarf, and gloves. Propelled by panic, I somehow reached the door and grasped the knob. I was unable to turn it. A wave of terror enveloped me, and I could feel my legs buckle.

Suddenly, I remembered advice from a former therapist— *"go to the center of the pain"*—advice that made no sense a year before. Stumbling back to the bed, I collapsed and begin to sob deep, wrenching, heart-breaking sobs. For the first time, I allowed the suffering to intensify and envelop me—I had no choice, no distractions. For the first time, I was unable to fight. The dam had broken. The agony, despair, and hopelessness were profound and complete. Trembling, I grasped my knees, rolled into a tight ball, and with a torrent of tears, an agonizing wail issued from the deepest part of my soul. In the midst of the suffering, seven little words surged into consciousness, echoing back through time: *"If I leave, they'll never find me."*

CHAPTER 5

◆ ◆ ◆ ◆ ◆

The Secret's in The Sensations:
Re-learning the Language of Mother Nature

With an eye made quiet by the power of harmony and the deep power of joy, we see into the life of things. *William Wordsworth*

Maligned by comics and rich fodder for late-night talk shows, the concept of "feelings" is greatly misunderstood, especially in Western industrialized cultures. Considered wussy, feminine, and weak, feelings have been equated with helplessness and a sense of impotence. Feelings are confused with behavior, with being impulsive, with being too sensitive, and with thoughts *about* feelings. But they are none of these.

Feelings are simply one's physical sensations. They are an innate feedback mechanism that provides vital and continuous information about your internal and external behavior and its effect on your well-being. Feelings alert you to potential danger, help you remember and make decisions, and provide a seamless connection to the outside world.

Feelings are the language of the system in which you live. They were your first language. You were born with them, and you will, hopefully, have them until the day you die. They are what tell you when you need to sleep, when you are getting sick or when you are getting well. If you are well attuned to them, they will tell you what to eat, when you are being manipulated or lied to, which decision to make, what career to pursue, and what partner to marry. Feelings are the language of the amygdala, of homeostasis, of Mother Nature. Their purpose is to keep you healthy, happy, and alive.

> Learn to listen. Opportunity could be knocking at your door very softly.
> —Frank Tyger

The Meaning of Feelings

Have you ever walked into the house after a long day, taken a deep breath, and let out a contented sigh? It's so good to be home, isn't it? That sigh was the sound of serenity. When you experience deep tranquility, you are where you are supposed to be. It is the voice of Mother Nature, giving you vital information for your well-being, telling you that when you're at peace, you're at home.

Unfortunately, most of us allow those moments to pass, virtually unnoticed. We fail to pay close attention to what caused the feeling, what preceded it, what that feeling was "about." We fail to note that we were pleased by a particular color, a sound, a vision. But the experiences that bring us deep pleasure, joy and tranquility are important. They are meant to be our guiding star leading us to shore, a magnet, shaping our lives and helping us appreciate ourselves as a unique piece of the universal puzzle.

Painful feelings are just as meaningful. Anxiety, depression, anger each carry a different and critical message as well as, believe it or not, detailed instructions for their dissolution. (The next chapter will delve into this subject in more detail.)

Most importantly, in order to understand where our distress comes from and how to get rid of it, we need to appreciate that, unlike behavior, feelings – be they serenity or pain – are never "wrong." And, unlike behavior, which is perfectly appropriate to suppress, they should be suppressed as rarely as possible.

> Unfortunately, more often than not, feelings – especially distressful or angry ones – don't mean what we think they mean at first blush. There is great danger in acting on them without first understanding exactly and accurately what they are trying to tell us.
> —The author

Our First Language

We were all born fully fluent in the language of feelings. Those who were encouraged to maintain their fluency are emotionally tranquil and serene. They are as aware of the stream of feelings that flow continuously through their body as they are of the parallel stream of thoughts that flows through their mind. They respond appropriately to the subtlest of their sensations instinctively and unconsciously. And for most of them, the process is so automatic they can't understand why you don't or even *that* you don't.

Unfortunately, for whatever reason – parents who did not respect your feelings, punishment for expressing them, a culture that emphasizes the superiority of rational thought – it is a language with which you may be no longer be familiar. You may be unaware of your feelings, especially the more subtle ones that constitute your intuition or inner voice. You may be completely oblivious to the difference between thoughts and feelings, as I was, or have conflicting feelings and not know which ones are "right." You may distrust your feelings, be confused, and not know what to do with them. You may think that your feelings are a mistake, and completely miss what they are trying to tell you.

Befriending Your Feelings

Feelings are experienced not as thoughts, but as physical sensations. They are *not* experienced in your head, where most people look, but in your body, which is why we have such expressions as "gut wrenching" experience and an "aching heart." They are not your thoughts *about* your feelings, but the physical sensations and the emotions that accompany them, the butterflies

> It is the spirit of the age to believe that any fact, no matter how suspect, is superior to any imaginative exercise, no mater how true.
> —Gore Vidal

in the tummy, the lump in the throat, the nervous bead of moisture that appears on the upper lip. They are the physical manifestation of the fear that you will make a fool of yourself, that no one will ever love you, that nothing you ever do is good enough. They are the sensation that you have known someone you just met, the sweaty palms you have before making a presentation, or the elation you feel when you see the one you love after a long absence.

One of the first and most critical steps in understanding what your feelings mean and getting rid of distress is to ask the question **What** *do I feel right now?* Do you feel anxious? Angry? Sad? Hopeless? These questions keep you in the amygdala or emotional brain and get you more familiar with it.

Instead of focusing on *what* we feel, however, we generally ask the "why" question – **Why** *do I feel this way?* obsessively thinking, searching for the origins, the reasons, the meaning of our feelings. We have the mistaken idea that if we can just figure out why we are so frightened or so sad or so angry, we won't feel that way any more. But to ask "why" is to revert back to the neocortex or rational brain which is not designed to handle emotional problems. As Dr. Michael Gazzaniga points out in *Nature's Mind*

> *our mind has an absurdly hard time when it tries to control our automatic brain. Turning off worry, for example. The conscious self is like a harried playground monitor with the responsibility of keeping track of multitudinous brain impulses running in all directions at once.*

The second series of questions is a bit more difficult, especially if you are not familiar with the nuances of feeling. Staying with your sensations as long as you need, ask exactly what are you afraid of? What do you feel is going to happen? Try to keep your focus on your body and what it is experiencing. You are looking for a bit more specific description of your feelings, the

> Follow your instincts. That's where true wisdom manifests itself.
> —*Oprah Winfrey*

"texture" of your feelings such as "I feel like I'm not good enough." "I feel as if the whole world is going to fall in on me." "I feel like the bottom is going to fall out." "I feel like I am going to die." I feel like no one will ever love me."

Take a moment right now and think of a person or event that is emotionally evocative for you – something that you think will cause a surge of physical feeling, something exquisitely joyful or extremely painful. Use your imagination and picture the person or event like a movie.

What came into your mind? Was it the physical description of the person, a replaying of the event, ideas about your self in the scenario? These are your thoughts.

Now, picture the same scene again, but this time, notice your emotions and put words on them. – are you experiencing joy, anxiety, pain, anger, depression or sadness? Take a moment right now and experience the emotion.

Did your mind zip back and forth, wondering why you feel the way you do, trying to figure out a way to stop feeling this way, wishing the other person would not act so badly? These are your thoughts *about* your feelings. They are not the same as your feelings.

Now, with the same scene in mind, focus on the body sensations that accompany your thoughts.

Are your muscles tense? Is there a lump forming in your throat? A stab in your heart? Is your stomach churning? Are your palms sweaty? Is your heart pounding? Are your nerves jittery? **These** are your feelings. They are the pure body sensations, *not* the interpretations we make from them.

Ask yourself exactly what the feeling of fear is saying to you. Do you fear death? Being abandoned? Being overwhelmed and suffocated? Do you feel as if you will be laughed at? Do you feel powerless? As though no matter what you do there is no way out? Do you feel the weight of the world on your shoulders? As if you are always alone with no one to help you? Be as specific as possible. This is a skill that you will need in order to follow the instructions in Part III and erase distress.

> The most beautiful thing we can experience is the mysterious. It is the source of all true art and all science. He to whom this emotion is a stranger, who can no longer pause to wonder and stand rapt in awe is as good as dead: his eyes are closed.
> —*Albert Einstein*

Now try to switch out of your feelings into your thoughts. Ask yourself the "why" question. Why do I feel this way? Why did they do that to me? How can I stop them? How can I stop feeling this way. See if you can get into the obsessive-thinking pattern with which you are probably familiar. Let the words spill out regarding the incident or the person that you have been focusing on. Were they unfair to you? Hostile or loving? Talk to yourself *about* the experience. This is being in the neocortex, the rational or verbal brain. It is *not* where you want to go if you want to get permanent relief from distress, anxiety and depression.

Switch back to your feelings again. Try to stop the obsessive thoughts by focusing on your body and its sensations. This is a skill you will use over and over again as you learn to switch from the language of words to the language of feelings. It will get you familiar with the difference between thoughts and feelings and give you experience turning off the neocortex and going into the amygdala.

How You Lost Them:

Feelings are reflected in every baby's cry, every gurgle, every smile, and every coo. If our parents responded appropriately to these messages, if they came when we cried, cuddled us and reinforced our smiles, we learned to trust our feelings as our guide, and our emotional brain, the amygdala, remained healthy. But if the messages were ignored or denigrated we learned to both be hypervigilant – scanning the environment for danger – and to discount our feelings in general.

> How much has to be explored and discarded before reaching the naked flesh of feeling.
> —*Claude Debussy*

Neglect can be a precipitating event, but there are many others as well. To respond to a child's outstretched arms with a brusque "later," or to pretend you didn't hear "come look at my painting" can be hurtful. To tell a toddler to "stop yer snivilin" when she needs comforting, to feed a newborn by the clock instead of his hunger, or to insist that a two-year-old not whine during a long shopping trip, are all damaging. Some children are slapped or beaten for the slightest offense. Others are told to "quit crying or I'll give you something to cry about."

"You shouldn't be mad," "that doesn't hurt," "you have no reason to dislike Uncle Herman," "you shouldn't feel that way," all separate us from the very mechanism that is designed to guide and protect us from harm. The message is clear: your feelings don't count. I don't want to hear about them.

> *The way I used to deal with feelings is I would put them down. I would downplay them if they didn't make sense to me, I would try to disregard them. I would try to rationalize them away. I would say all the time I shouldn't be feeling this way. This doesn't make any sense. I was always trying to use reason. Trying to reason my emotions. Trying to use logic. I believed they weren't important. I definitely suppressed them. I tried to hide them. I tried to stuff them in different ways.*

What happened in your family of origin? Did family members generally respect each other's feelings? Or did they act as if some of your feelings were wrong? Did you get the subtle or overt message that you weren't supposed to feel a certain way, or, at the least, you weren't supposed to say what you felt? Negating someone else's sensations – telling them they don't really feel something, is common. But, believing that our feelings and physical sensations, these products of the amygdala, are a mistake is like thinking there is something wrong with our need for food or sleep. Feelings are our internal compass. Disregarding them, ignoring them, or suppressing them destroys the internal self. Regardless of the cause, disconnecting from feelings seriously compromises the emotional immune system and is at the core of virtually all emotional distress and much of our physical illness, family dysfunction and social unrest as well.

Co-dependence and Sensations

Not knowing what you feel, being unaware of the sensations that are your inner voice and therefore needing to rely on others for direction is the cause of and very definition of co-dependence.

Picture yourself traveling in a rocket to the moon when you lose the delicate guidance mechanism in the rocket's nose cone. You are tumbling through the atmosphere without the instruments you so desperately need, frightened, spacey, lost.

"Ground control, ground control," you scream. "Come in, come in."

"This is ground control," comes the reply.

"I've lost the guidance mechanism," you tell them. "I don't know where I am or where I am headed. Help!"

And so, ground control takes over your rocket, and you are relieved to have them do so. They may safely get you to your destination or not, but they are your only hope. The fact is, your fate is in their hands. It is no longer in your own.

It is understandable that under those circumstances you would need others and fear that they might leave. Dependent on others for your very survival, you would be easy to manipulate and would likely "put up with" disrespect and bad behavior from others. If ground control has command of the instruments, you would naturally see them as more powerful than you and feel the need to accede to their wishes to ensure your safety.

These are the same characteristics that define co-dependent behavior. Unaware of our most subtle feelings, we are also separated from our innate guidance mechanism, reliant on other's opinions, their decisions, and their preferences.

> Most mental health professionals are untreated co-dependents who are actively participating in their disease in their work in a way that helps neither them nor their clients.
> —Anne Wilson Schaef

We call friends and ask what we should do. We are threatened by abandonment and feel alone. We ask for advice, read self-help books, and rely on experts to prescribe our diet, our clothing styles, our career choices, our home décor or our child-rearing behavior.

Because we are so unaware of our inner sensations, we are also blind to our own unique character and where we belong in the world. We read celebrity magazines, find out what the elite are doing and follow the latest trends. We wear brown lipstick though it may clash with our coloring, because it's "in," and buy a more expensive car than we can afford so that we "look good" to others. Those who are still in touch with their inner guidance system get their sense of self-worth from their deeds and from the "ahhhh" feeling that comes from knowing that they are in the right place, when things just "feel right." Without those sensations, confidence must come from outside, from others. And it can be taken away at any moment.

Sensitivity and Sense Ability

Some of you may now be saying, "But I am too sensitive. I react to everything and everybody. I need to be less sensitive, not more. But there is a vast difference between being sense-able – that is, to be able to sense and interpret the meaning of one's most subtle feelings – and to be sensitive, that is, to react emotionally to external events and people.

To be sense-able is to have a finely tuned emotional immune system, to be aware of the slightest deviation from normal and to take corrective action before it grows. Physically, it is the same as being aware that you are slightly more tired than usual and that unless you rest you will be sick the next day.

To react with distress to external events, however, is a sign of an ongoing emotional infection.

CHAPTER 6

♦ ♦ ♦ ♦ ♦

"Old Stuff"
Catching an Emotional Infection

Be quiet and then you begin to see with the eye of the heart.
Desmond Tutu

His diaries and letters are saturated with rage, with diatribes against anyone who might attempt to control him, with treatises against the tyranny of technology, and with frequent fantasies of revenge.   For many years he was not able to express his fury openly because . . . "I was too strongly conditioned . . . against any defiance of authority."

Often angry, he despises people in positions of power—psychiatrists, politicians, dictators, businessmen, scientists, communists—anyone who might attempt to control him. "Organized society" he says, "frustrates my very powerful urge for physical freedom and personal autonomy."

He believes that society's reach is rapidly expanding and fears it will eventually obliterate individual liberty. He is especially concerned about propaganda, education, conditioning, direct physical control of emotions via electrodes and "chemitrodes," biofeedback training, memory pills, drugs, and genetic engineering. Even his dreams are filled with hate and fear. He writes,

During my years at Michigan I occasionally began having dreams of a type that I continued to have occasionally over a period of several years. In the dream I would feel either that organized society was hounding me with accusation in some way, or that organized society was trying in some way to capture my mind and tie me down psychologically or both. In the most typical form some psychologist or psychologists (often in association with parents or other minions of the system) would either be trying to convince me that I was "sick" or would be trying to control my mind through psychological techniques.

I would be on the dodge, trying to escape or avoid the psychologist either physically or in other ways. But I would grow angrier and finally I would break out in physical violence against the psychologist and his allies.

At the moment when I broke out into violence and killed the psychologist or other such figure, I experienced a great feeling of relief and liberation. Unfortunately, however, the people I killed usually would spring back to life again very quickly. They just wouldn't stay dead. I would awake with a pleasurable sense of liberation at having broken into violence, but at the same time with some frustration at the fact that my victims wouldn't stay dead

However, in the course of some dreams, by making a strong effort of will in my sleep, I was able to make my victims stay dead. I think that, as the years went by, the frequency with which I was able to make my victims stay dead through exertion of will increased.

"He believes that the technological society or system is out to harm him," said his brother sadly, "and, as painful as it is, that his family is bent on hurting him." But he had a normal childhood, everyone agrees. His father was a sausage maker, a man with extensive community activities and many friends; his mother, a homemaker for much of his childhood, and later a teacher. His brother, seven years younger, and he were close. Even in an autobiography written in 1959, he describes an uneventful early childhood, indicates that he was somewhat rebellious towards his parents, who were quite lenient with him, and describes their relationship as affectionate.

It is true, as was common in those days, that the family didn't talk much about feelings; problems were generally ignored after everyone simmered down. But, almost in compensation, it was a highly intellectual home with frequent conversations about politics, philosophy and current events, discussions enjoyed by a boy with an IQ of 170 who would graduate from Harvard at the age of twenty.

But then there was that picture, that awful, unforgettable, horrific picture.

Someone at the hospital captured the tearless terror in the 10-month-old infant's eyes. Hospital personnel had restrained the baby, pinned him down spread-eagle style to examine a rash when the picture was taken. Over the next eight months, there would be a number of other admissions for the same persistent problem. But as with the first hospitalization, his mother was not allowed to visit him. *"Baby home from hospital and is healthy, but quite unresponsive after his experience,"* his mother wrote in his 1943 baby book. Soon she noticed emotional "shutdowns" often accompanied by rage and wondered if they were somehow related to the hospitalizations.

Fifty years later, a defiant Theodore Kaczynski, proclaiming his desire to kill "high" persons and save humanity from the ravages of technology, was arrested.

"My motive for doing what I am going to do is simply personal revenge," the Unabomber stated flatly about his plans for killing.

For reasons we will never know—fear of authority, unparalleled despair from having his cries ignored, or both—by the time the infamous picture was taken, this ten-month-old infant could not express his agony. With a force of will that can only be considered exceptional, he held in his terror and anger at the people who were responsible for it. And there it lay, festering, for fifty years

The Past Infects the Present

Ted Kaczynski's experience as a baby may be extreme, but it is a textbook example of how unexpressed traumatic memories that are stored in the amygdala can lie in wait until triggered by similar events in the here and now. The process is the same for all of us.

♦ Janice becomes agitated when her boyfriend is late and upset if he pays attention to anyone else at a party. Janice's mother deserted the family when she was 6; her father was very distraught, and somehow, Janice, instead of being comforted, became the comforter.

♦ Roger feels suffocated and becomes furious whenever his wife innocently asks him where he is going and when he will be back. His childhood home was strained, his parents estranged, and his mother overly protective and doting.

♦ When Tiffany asks Brian if he could be a bit more careful with his language around her daughter, he sulks for hours rather than cheerfully complying. Brian's parents were extremely critical and even now as an adult he perceives a reproach in every request.

♦ When Sally is laid off from her job, she falls apart. She feels useless, not valued, as if she had done something wrong, the same feeling she experienced as a child.

Why are psychiatrists' couches filled with people who carry the burdens of emotional and sexual abuse decades after it occurred? The answer to this question is critical, because while emotional memories of this kind are

> Until the old moon disappears completely, the new moon can not come.
> —Bahunde Proverb

notoriously intractable in human beings, they are less resistant to extinction in animals, even those that are traumatized. How, given our superior intellect and massive resources, could this possibly be? What does the animal kingdom know that we don't? Lets take a look at the trauma process as nature intended.

The 4 F's: Fright, Fight, Flight, Freeze

Both human beings and animals are equipped with a complex and impressive system that helps them both survive threats and recover from stress.

The moment an animal or human being perceives danger it mobilizes its internal forces to help it prevail against whatever danger it faces. The body is flooded with adrenaline and noradrenaline, the bronchial tubes expand, breathing accelerates, digestion stops and oxygen pours into the brain and muscles. The heart begins to beat faster, blood pressure rises, and blood flows away from the extremities into the core of the body to protect them from potential blood loss. These physiological responses occur in a deer stalked by a lion, in a child facing a whipping, in an adult confronting a robber.

The choices facing the organism at that moment are three. It can fight back. It can attempt to flee. Or, if neither of these options is available, it may freeze – as occurs when a deer is caught in the headlights of an oncoming car, or a child hides under the covers from scary noises, for example. Then, when the danger is over, an animal will innately release the tension that was stored and its body will return to normal. In the wild, a deer can be seen shaking and trembling as the nervous system gradually slows the heart and breathing, lowers the blood pressure and returns the digestive process to its pre-crisis levels.

The same process is supposed to, and often does occur in humans. We can all probably remember at least one instance in which we faced an emergency, responded heroically, and then fell apart. Perhaps there was a fire, and you ran through the house gathering the children, your prized possessions, a fire extinguisher or called 911. Afterward, you may have trembled, been overcome with chills, or perhaps you sobbed uncontrollably. The same kind of scenario may have played itself out after an automobile accident. You may have been shaken and weak. These are all normal and necessary physiological responses that allow the body to respond aggressively, cope with an emergency and yet return to a state of health and well being.

This process operates even during the night, as nature tries to dissolve emotional trauma through your dreams.

Recovery Interrupted

So, how does the process go wrong? With rare exceptions, it doesn't for animals. Dominated by his instincts, the animal must cooperate with homeostasis and the immune system.

But there is no such mandate for human beings. We can overrule our desire to cry by "sucking it up," distracting ourselves, or drowning in beer, stop ourselves from shaking or trembling by sheer force of will and the desire to appear powerful, and even delay the body's need for sleep with caffeine, amphetamines. Unlike animals, human beings are uniquely capable of suppressing and thereby compromising the natural process of homeostasis and thus derailing Mother Nature. We can suppress so much emotional "stuff" during the day that nature is unable to discharge it even during our nighttime dreams. We do it all the time, especially those of us who were raised in homes in which our most subtle sensations were not understood or respected, or where withholding feelings was a survival tactic.

- ◆ Sarah cowered under the covers whenever she heard her father staggering up the stairs. Terrified that he would molest her, she prayed silently and pretended to be asleep.

- ◆ Jason wore a cloak of masculine bravado as he detailed his confrontation with the armed burglar to the police, his wife and his friends, and even himself. It was nothing, he tells himself. Only a wimp feels fear.

- ◆ When Derek's father first began to whip him, Derek cried. But when Derek realized his father was infuriated by the tears and beat him even harder, he learned to face the lashing with steely cold anger.

And this is where the problem begins.

CHAPTER 7

♦ ♦ ♦ ♦ ♦

Repression
The Infection Worsens

Resistance drains energy. Acceptance saves it. Cheerfulness
sustains it. *Anonymous.*

As a small child, he was neglected. He and his two siblings,
in essence, raised themselves. His parents, cold and aloof,
showed no affection and little emotion for each other or
toward the children. His mother, a disorganized chatterbox was
usually in bed when he left for school, and invariably gone by the
time he returned. His father worked long hours and engaged in a
number of adulterous relationships on the side. His family rode a
financial roller coaster and his parent's marriage finally dissolved
with little fanfare.

He was the brightest and eldest of three, anxious and miserable and
worn beyond his years. As a dependent child, like all children, he
quite naturally needed to feel loved and valued, hugged and kissed

and cared for. But that was not the way in his family, and so, by the tender age of five he quite deliberately and consciously decided that he would abandon his "childish" need for affection and attention, stop complaining about his lot in life and make the best of a difficult situation. He cut off the unpleasant feelings of yearning for something he could never have, with thinking and willpower.

He faced serious childhood illness with the same iron resolve. Although hospitalized several times between the ages of five and seven, his parents rarely visited and he was left to fend for himself. Unprepared for a painful operation, he at first developed fantasies of revenge, but in the end, suppressed his fear and looked upon that event and other painful invasive medical procedures with disengaged scientific interest.

He shut himself off not only from his own feelings but from those around him as well. He was rebellious in college, easily irritated by stupidity and especially intolerant of his sister's inability to exhibit the fortitude he had perfected. Asked to reflect on his experience with employers, he never acknowledged his need for them or any affection either. They were important only in regards to what they could do for him.

His sexual attitude and behavior appears to have developed at the same time he started to squelch his emotions. He was caught in bed with a childhood friend, Ruthie, at the precocious age of five (an act he believed his parents secretly admired), and had fantasies of making love to a girl he met in the hospital about the same time.

His adult relationships were characterized by extreme emotions, co-dependence and promiscuity. At 24 he fell in love with Karyl, a woman encumbered with an abusive boyfriend, once writing her a 99-page letter. A 20-year affair with Gertrude, whom he could never manage to marry, lasted through her two marriages.

Despite four years of intensive psychoanalysis, he was plagued by a germ phobia, insomnia, fits of rage, spates of vulgar language, and the inability to apologize for his even most outlandish outbursts. Though he denies he was influenced by the hidden hurts of his childhood, he is, according to his biographer, dogmatic, insensitive, and disagreeable, a workaholic and a loner who craves influence, power, a sense of importance, and, above all, an audience.

Professionally, he is the father of Rational Emotive Behavior Therapy, a popular approach to psychology that advocates thought control as the ultimate answer to emotional turmoil. Convinced that people are disturbed by what they *think* about their problems rather than the feelings about the problems themselves, Albert Ellis advises suppression of uncomfortable emotions and disturbing thoughts.

Sanity, Ellis believes, is the absence of troubling emotions, something, he reluctantly admits, is difficult for human beings. In his view, the ultimate achievement in life is to be rational, scientific, hedonistic, and in control – in essence, to suppress feelings. He is the penultimate Cartesian-Newtonian model

Repression, Pretense and Reality

Albert Ellis's biography provides a rare glimpse into the mind of a child who made painful feelings the enemy, and the man who made a career of teaching others to do the same. Now, it is true that the ability to retain rather than express what you feel is an important skill. After all, just because you feel like screaming in the middle of the mall

> Not everything that is faced can be changed, but nothing can be changed until it is faced.
> —James Baldwin

doesn't mean the little green men in the starched white coats won't haul you off to the funny farm with their big blue nets!

Repression is particularly handy in an emergency: you can stay cool until a crisis is over and *then* fall apart. Or when you are angry and your first impulse is to take your fury out on someone or something else. And it is critical when we are talking about controlling behavior (in this case, one might wish for more repression!). Repression is also useful when we are teaching children to delay gratification. One of the most powerful predictors of a child's future success is his or her ability to not eat one marshmallow now in order to get two later.

But for many people, families, and cultures, the idea that feelings should be routinely suppressed, repressed, thwarted, overcome, and manipulated by our thoughts, chemicals or sheer willpower is rampant. Storing rather than expressing feelings is a way of life. Stuffing the pain is what one is supposed to do. Geraldine is aware that if she cries when her mother hits her, she will be hit even harder. Zachary knows that to earn his father's approval he needs to be strong and stalwart, never letting on how much the cutting remarks hurt. Cecilia is afraid that if she tells her parents how she feels, they will get angry and yell. David is afraid that if he tells his mother to stop smothering him, she will withdraw her love and protection from him forever.

> He knows the universe and does not know himself.
> —Jean De La Fontaine

> *Before I attended the Turmoil to Tranquility seminar I certainly had a lot of feelings. They were bad feelings, and my way of dealing with them was to do whatever I could to subdue them so I really wouldn't have to face them, so I could overpower them with my own thinking about ways to deal with the feelings.*

In such environments, emotional distress is saved up, experience by experience instead of being naturally dissipated by the innate process of homeostasis. By the time one reaches adulthood, there is a mountain of stored traumatic memories, like a stack of plates in a cafeteria, waiting to be removed, one by one. And, because Mother Nature meant for the ability to repress to be short-term rather than long, they do considerable damage.

> *A golf-ball sized lump in the throat was my constant companion. I swallowed constantly in an attempt to push it down, but of course, it didn't go anywhere. Occasionally, especially if I was able to work at home, I poured myself a small glass of wine and nursed it for several hours, sipping just enough to keep the lump at bay, but not so much that I couldn't focus on my work.*

But make no mistake about it. There is a great deal of difference between pretending we don't feel something and not feeling it. Stuffing the dirty clothes under the bed is not the same as doing the laundry. Taking a pain-killer and ignoring the pain in your chest is not identical to getting a heart bypass. Just because you disconnect the warning lights on the dashboard of your car doesn't mean that the car is somehow in tip-top condition. Just because you pretend to be healthy doesn't mean you actually are. *Ignoring warning signals is dangerous.*

Charles Nemeroff of Emory University in Atlanta and author of a study of childhood abuse of girls has concluded that early abuse can alter a woman's brain chemistry, changing her response to stress and increasing the risk of mood and anxiety disorders later in life. The study offers the first evidence in humans that early trauma can have lasting effects on the brain. Other studies have documented shrinkage of the hippocampus and amygdala, damaged memory, altered brain neurons, and damage to neurotransmitters and their receptors amongst those who have experienced PTSD (post traumatic stress disorder). How does this happen? Thanks to recent brain imaging techniques such as PET scans and fMRI's, we have new insight into why and how this process works.

The Biology of Memory

Human beings are blessed with at least two different memory systems. The first, the hippocampus, processes *facts* about events – both those that are emotionally evocative and those that are not. In the second, the amygdala processes and stores the chemicals of the actual *emotion* that was experienced during the event. It appears that when these emotional memories are not fully expressed and dissipated, they undergo protein synthesis in the amygdala and enter long-term storage.

These distressful memories act as foreign bodies in the brain. New fMRI studies show that each time an old emotional memory is triggered by an event in the here and now, they become labile – unstable, and subject to change. In the same way it strives to expel a splinter in the finger, or tainted food from the stomach and intestines, it seems that the body may be trying to dissolve the chemicals and hormones of old emotional pain and return the brain to a physiologically and psychologically healthy state.

If you attempt to repress the feeling instead of allowing it to emerge and dissipate, however, the memory appears again to undergo another protein synthesis and is re-stored in the brain. The process occurs over and over again as new memories are stored, and as old memories are triggered. It is as if the environment is always trying to take the emotional tape recorder off pause and replay the original feeling.

As long as it remains in storage, the original trauma, though long past, will continue to do its damage. Like a low grade fever, too generalized and diffuse to identify, emotional infections weaken our emotional resilience, sapping our ability to withstand additional emotional experiences.

For those who have stuffed the most sensations, for those who may have endured multiple traumas and have kept it all wrapped tightly inside for the longest period of time, the environment becomes a source of significant discomfort. Everything, it seems, "reminds them" of the original experience. Everything seems to evoke the stored traumas. They become hypervigilant – always on the lookout for the next disaster.

The triggers do not have to be a perfect match with the original experience to provoke it, The relationship is not intellectual. It is physical and emotional. A friend's tardiness can evoke feelings of abandonment; a simple request, feelings of inferiority.

For Ted Kaczynsky, whom court psychiatrists labeled paranoid, such a trigger might be anything that "smacks" of hi-tech, or reminds him of the hospital equipment that was the instrument of his torture. Even isolation in a cabin in Montana was not sufficient to weaken his feelings of fear and anger to threats of control thousands of miles away. Normal attempts to control behavior, attempts that to the rest of us are minor and necessary for smooth social conduct, are likely to bring flooding back the anger and fear he felt at being restrained by hospital personnel.

A client recently told me:

> *When David would call me stupid and say I don't know anything and that everything is just fine and that he is fine and that I don't need to worry about anything, it reminded me of my mother. Because my mother would pretty much say the same things. Don't worry about me, I'm fine. Because I'm in control and you're not. Don't control me.*

> *That was really big – that was in my face. What's interesting is that growing up my mother had places and spots all over the house where she had bottles. Hatboxes, things I used to like to play with as a little kid. And I would find these bottles sometimes.*

> *It so turns out that David did the exact same thing. But they weren't just in the house. They were in the yard. They were in*

the toilet tank. I would find them in places where I least expected it. And then he would forget about it, and I would stumble across it, and . . . it was the same thing with my mother.

In one long-term study done in England, a group of children was followed to determine the effects of the World War II bombings of London on their future emotional health. The study discovered that children who were allowed to cry during the raids and were comforted by their caregivers grew up to be emotionally healthy. But those who were told not to cry, to hide their feelings and be strong, grew up with multiple neuroses, fractured careers, financial disarray, and multiple marriages. Although each group of children had had the same experience—all had endured multiple bombing raids in the underground shelters—the effects were vastly different.

This study and many others suggests that the key element in the ability to "get over" the effects of childhood trauma, centers not so much on the original experience itself, as on the role of repression. Those who expressed their feelings were healthy as adults; those who did not became "neurotic."

What are your triggers? What kinds of events and people flood you with emotional distress – fear, anxiety, anger or sadness? Begin to be aware of what they are and what they remind you of. What themes emerge? Do you fear abandonment or engulfment?

> Darkness cannot drive out darkness, only light can do that.
> —*Martin Luther King*

Do you feel out of control? Or do you fear being controlled? Being criticized or ignored? These are the keys to your old stored memories.

It's Always "Old Stuff"

And, how do we know if it's "old stuff" when we are emotionally distressed? It's almost *always* old stuff. Unless we are talking about something as random as a drive-by shooting, if it's emotionally evocative, if it's uncomfortable, if it hurts, if you feel like a victim, at its core, it's old stuff. "Old stuff" is involved whenever there is anxiety, fear, depression, anger, jealousy, blame, phobias, flashbacks, or obsessive-compulsive behavior. It is involved whenever we feel like running away or lashing out, when we want to avoid confrontation, or feel like the "other" is more powerful than we. It is involved in a myriad of social disorders— divorce, child abuse, addictions, suicide, and much of our crime. It is always involved when we are trying to control someone else, when we lie, when we manipulate, when we are afraid to deal openly and honestly with others.

This phenomenon need not be as obvious as it was with Ted Kaczynsky. It can occur under

> Nothing is so easy as to deceive one's self; for what we wish, that we readily believe.
> —*Demosthenes*

the most innocuous and seemingly unrelated circumstances:

♦ When Amy sold her house, she generously filled and repainted all the picture holes in the walls, saved and labeled paint samples, and made arrangements to have the carpets shampooed. When the buyers made a few last minute but petty demands, she flew into rage. At the bottom of the anger was the old feeling "no matter what I do it isn't good enough."

♦ After losing a court battle over a speeding ticket in which the police officer lied under oath, Eric, who found out by accident when he was eight that he was adopted, was visibly upset. At the core of the pain was the old feeling "how could they have lied to me?"

♦ Kay's ownership of a rented condo was troublesome from the start. When her multiple attempts to dislodge the disagreeable tenant resulted in failure, Kay was desolate. The feeling it aroused was "I'm all alone. There is never anyone there to help me."

And it can be all-encompassing.

A couple of years ago everything would trigger me. Dripping water from the shower would trigger me. Now of course, it doesn't trigger me. People would trigger me with what they said. I took everything personally. I felt controlled and trapped, at the slightest drop of a hat, I would want to run.

I was afraid even of my feelings. I was afraid of doing or saying the wrong things. I was afraid to get hurt. I was afraid to hurt others. I was just fearful – anything would set me off. Anything. The door closing. Somebody tapping on my back which would cause me to jump out of my skin.

"But if Jeff would call when he is late, if he would try harder to be on time, I wouldn't get upset," protested Ginger. "Life would be smoother, and I would feel fine." Perhaps, but only temporarily. Jeff is not "causing" Ginger's turmoil, he is only triggering it. The feeling belongs to Ginger; it is something she stuffed at some point in her life. As soon as she erases it, Jeff's tardiness will cease to upset her.

Virtually all the emotional turmoil we feel and the physical discomfort that accompanies it is Mother Nature with a simple message: there is an old emotional infection somewhere in your body and it wants to come out. But, trusting our thoughts more than our feelings, suspicious of nature and unaware of the process of homeostasis, most of us show blatant disregard for the signals of the body. Instead of addressing the problem and correcting it, we focus our attention on the suppression of pain.

CHAPTER 8

◆ ◆ ◆ ◆ ◆

The Positive Purpose of Pain
A Cry from the Therapist Within™

If you could read the secret history of our enemies, we should find in each man's life, sorrow and suffering enough to disarm all hostility. *Henry Wadsworth Longfellow*

Unfortunately, we misunderstand the experience of pain as much as we do the concept of feelings. We don't interpret our distress as a symptom with a clear message because it doesn't tell us in words what to do. And so, not knowing, we focus virtually all our attention on getting rid of it.

- ◆ The average American consumes 250 aspirin a year
- ◆ One third of all drugs sold are designed to suppress the central nervous system

♦ The three top selling drugs in the country are for hypertension, ulcers, and a tranquilizer.

♦ Pain relief in the US is now a $63-billion-dollar-a-year industry

This approach to pain is endemic. But, by spending so much time and energy trying to kill pain instead of changing our circumstances, we actually prolong and deepen it. We make pain the enemy, when it is actually our friend, one of our best friends. A friend we need to get to know.

Physical and Psychic Pain Are One

Contrary to popular opinion, there is no significant separation between mind and body. Only those of us who are cut off from our most subtle feelings can possibly believe there is a difference between physical and psychic pain.

Take a moment right now to imagine a distressful event. Close your eyes and picture it like a moving picture. Note where the discomfort arises first. Is it in your chest? Your breathing? Do you have butterflies in your stomach or is there a growing lump in your throat? How about tightness in the forehead?

These feelings are caused by your nervous and endocrine systems engaged in a complex dance that prepares you for emergencies and afterward restores you to health. When you are faced with a crisis – whether it is real – occurring in the here and now – or a memory that is being triggered, the response is the same. Your heart beats faster, your blood pressure increases, pupils dilate, the skin sweats, your lungs expand and digestion is inhibited. At the same time, hormones such as adrenaline, noradrenaline, and corticosteroids pour into the body. These physical changes are life-enhancing in the short run, but they do significant damage when the stress becomes chronic. But,

> Silence the pain and destroy the body or listen to the pain and preserve the body.
> —Dr. Paul Brand

regardless if the crisis is a one-time experience or ongoing, emotional distress is as real a physiological experience as is physical pain. In fact, it *is* physical pain with a message: stop damaging your body!

Pain Is a Gift

Though it might seem idyllic to live a pain free life, the fact is, you would be dead without discomfort. Pain is not the enemy. It is, instead, one of the most extraordinary aspects of the human body, an essential tool not only for our individual survival but for survival of the species as well.

> Don't be afraid your life will end;
> be afraid that it will never begin.
> —Grace Hansen

In *Pain, the Gift Nobody Wants*, Dr. Paul Brand tells the story of four-year old Tanya, an impish child suffering from "congenital indifference to pain," a rare genetic defect that left her without the ability to feel or respond appropriately to pain. Her mother first noticed something was wrong when she left her eighteen-month-old daughter in the playpen while she went to prepare dinner.

> *A few minutes later, I went into Tanya's room and found her sitting on the floor of the playpen finger painting red swirls on the white plastic sheet. I didn't grasp the situation at first, but when I got closer, I screamed. It was horrible. The tip of Tanya's finger was mangled and bleeding and it was her own blood she was using to make those designs on the sheets.*
>
> *I yelled, "Tanya, what happened!" She grinned at me and that's when I saw the streaks of blood on her teeth. She had bitten off the tip of her finger and was playing in the blood.*

Now, at four, Tanya's fingers were shortened and her feet were covered with infected ulcers. Her left ankle was dislocated, but no one could convince her not to walk on it. She was oblivious to pain.

Certainly as she grew up and could follow directions, Tanya should have stopped injuring herself. But no. Without a miracle that could restore Tanya's ability to feel unpleasantness, without medicine to restore her ability to protect herself, the prognosis was dim. Seven years later, Dr. Brand received a call from Tanya's mother. Tanya, now eleven and institutionalized, had lost most of her fingers, both her legs, and suffered from chronic sores on most of the surfaces of her body.

Pain Is a Request for Change, Not Punishment

Dr. Brand found the same phenomena with adults suffering from leprosy and diabetes—diseases that cause numbness in the extremities. Without pain, patients' extremities suffered injuries that they did not take care of. To correct the problem, Dr. Brand and his clinic developed electronic gloves that warned the wearer when they were putting too much pressure in a particular area. Dr. Brand writes:

> But when a patient with a damaged hand turned a
> screwdriver too hard, and the loud warning signal went off,
> he would simply override it . . . and turn the screwdriver
> anyway. . . Being alerted to the danger was not enough;
> our patients had to be forced to respond.

Adding shock to the system didn't work either. Most of the volunteers dropped out of the program. Those who didn't

> viewed pain from our artificial sensors in a different way
> than pain from natural sources. They tended to see the
> electric shocks as punishment for breaking rules, not as
> messages from an endangered body part. They responded
> with resentment, not an instinct for self-preservation

because our artificial system had no innate link to their sense of self.

Much to Dr. Brand's sorrow, the pain project failed. Science could not develop a better system than did nature.

Distress is often a request for the environment to change. When a child, dependent on others for its well being, cries, it announces that there is something wrong with how he is being treated, something not in her best interests. It is the language of Mother Nature asking the family

> You will not grow if you sit in a beautiful flower garden, But you will grow if you are sick, If you are in pain, if you experience losses, And if you do not put your head in the sand, But take the pain as a gift to you with a very, very specific purpose.
> —*Elizabeth Kubler Ross*

and the community to pay attention, to do something to care for the child. It is the only way an infant has to assure its survival. It's intent is to change the milieu, to make the environment healthier.

Most Pain Is a Symptom of Healing

But discomfort does more than alert us to danger and encourage us to create a more hospitable environment. Most discomfort, in fact, comes not from disease, but from our body's attempts to fight the disease. Redness, swelling, fever are our immune system in action. They tell us that our white blood cells are on the job and that the body is mobilizing its forces to make the environment unpleasant for the invading enemy.

The swelling of a pimple announces its imminent discharge and seeks a hot compress. The irritation around a splinter asks that we squeeze it or tweeze it as soon as it breaks the skin's surface. The

> In the depth of winter, I finally learned that within me there lay an invincible summer.
> —*Albert Camus*

sniffles or a sore throat announce that our body's defenses are preparing to fight a virus invader and asks us to rest, to sleep more, to protect ourselves from other infections or trauma. Though these events may be uncomfortable, if we look at them realistically, we will see that they are comforting as well. Soon it will be over. Soon the splinter will come out, the pimple will discharge its poison, the sore throat will be gone.

Emotional turmoil is nature's way of telling us that there is an infection that is getting ready to be expelled, her way of getting our attention, of letting us know there is an important healing process going on. It announces that we are on the precipice of health and begs our cooperation.

> Wisdom ceases to be wisdom when it becomes too proud to weep, too grave to laugh, and too selfful to seek other than itself.
> —Kahlil Gibran

> *I'm finding that feeling my old stored emotions is becoming much easier. It is my struggle to keep them from coming up that caused me so much pain.*

> *When I finally feel the original feeling I think, "gees Maureen, that wasn't so bad why did I give myself such a hard time just getting there in the first place???" I'm really getting that the feelings are nothing compared to the resistance I put up to stop myself from feeling.*

Pain Is Only As Bad As It Needs To Be To Get Your Attention

Both physical and emotional distress are designed specifically to be only so uncomfortable that they *must* be attended to and can't be ignored. They tell us, in Dr. Brand's words

> *Listen to your body, and above all, listen to your pain. It may be trying to tell you that you are violating your brain with tension, your ears with loudness, your eyes with constant television, your stomach with unhealthy food, your lungs with cancer-producing pollutants. Listen carefully to*

the message of pain before I give you something to relieve those symptoms. I can help with the symptoms, but you must address the cause.

The positive purpose of pain is to get your attention and save your life. If you are alert to the first twinge and take the appropriate corrective action, distress subsides. If, instead, you ignore it or try to push it away, it will grow into an 800 pound gorilla, threatening to take over your life.

> Never mistake knowledge for wisdom. One helps you make a living, the other helps you make a life.
> —*Sandra Carey*

Discomfort alerts us to unhealthy ways of living, distracts us from our daily routine, and demands that we change what we are doing. If we don't change, it becomes louder and more insistent. Because physical and emotional discomfort are both located in the body, they work to change our behavior in precisely the same way.

- A sharp stab in his back tells Marc to stand and bend in a different way

- Janie's tears tells her mother to feed her or change her diaper

- The pain of losing Polly Klass convinced legislators to tighten the penalties for habitual criminals.

A few years ago I had lunch with "The Candidate for Political Office" at the request of one of his supporters. Handsome, successful, with a photogenic family and connections in high places "The Candidate" had run for office twice before. And had lost. Twice. During each of his previous campaigns, something had triggered his anger and he had gone on a partisan tirade in front of the press.

This time, however, everyone was sure it would be different. "The Candidate," a moderate in a centrist district, was way ahead of the pack for the primary, and sure to win against the opposing party in the general election. The primary was just a week or two away when I met with him.

His anger was palpable. It simmered just beneath the surface until the topic turned to President Clinton, the scandals, and the unrelenting conservative attacks. "The reason," I offered, "that Clinton's ratings went up the more the conservatives trashed him was because most citizens wanted politicians to do the country's business and were turned off by distracting partisan behavior."

There ensued a diatribe against the President, his personal foibles, and lies. The hatred was intense and personal. I suggested that it was possible to disagree with the President's policies, even with his behavior without anger, but "The Candidate's" response was an even greater explosion. The President, he hissed, was completely immoral, and the Democrat landslide was the only reason "The Candidate" had lost the last election.

I knew without a doubt that his anger was old stuff, and that it was going to destroy any hope of a political career. Before the lunch ended, I suggested that anger was something he might want to deal with, that the way the universe worked is to first send us a pebble. If we paid no attention, it sent us a rock. And if we still ignored it, it sent us a boulder. "The Candidate" politely informed me that this wasn't the way the universe worked, and I was dismissed. He had been through two losing campaigns already; he had already received his pebble and rock. I was concerned about a looming boulder.

A few days later I went on a lengthy vacation. Upon my return, I opened the newspaper to see his face – and a local scandal. It seems that just days before the primary, "The Candidate" had been accused of tearing down the signs of his opponents in the middle of the night. Asked by the press if he had done so, he emphatically denied it, insisting he had been home in bed with his wife that night, and telling the press to "just ask her," in pure Gary-Hart-style. Unfortunately for him, however, he had been videotaped doing a war dance while tearing the signs into shreds. His anger over the fact that his opponent's signs were slightly larger than regulation size had capsized his campaign. "The Candidate's" career in politics was over. He got his boulder.

> Our real blessings often appear to us in the shapes of pains, losses and disappointments; but let us have patience, and we soon shall see them in their proper figures.
> —*Joseph Addison*

Pain and Narcissism

A discussion of pain would not be complete without addressing the issue of narcissism. The accusation of narcissism, of being wrapped up in and concerned only with oneself, is often flung in the direction of those who are in emotional turmoil. Many biographies of Princess Diana point to narcissism as one of her least attractive qualities. Many of us have friends who are always bending our ear with their latest travail. This is a confusing issue for people who are trying to deal with their pain *and* please everyone around them at the same time. How can I be narcissistic when I am continually focused on the well being of my family and friends, they ask. But this confuses the issue of narcissism. There is actually good narcissism and bad narcissism

When one is in pain, one is supposed to be narcissistic. The purpose of pain is to be so uncomfortable that we will lay aside our other concerns, pay attention and solve whatever problem lies in front of us. If you are a parent flying to Paris and there is a change in cabin pressure, you are supposed to put on your own oxygen mask first and then attend to the children. We are biologically made to attend to pain, make ourselves well, so that we are able to truly attend to others. Narcissism is about the organism crying for attention and fighting for its survival. It is a symptom. You are supposed to pay attention—if you don't, the pain will just get worse.

Attending to everyone's needs but your own is bad narcissism.
Though we may believe we are being unselfish when we cater to
everyone else's needs other than our own, what we are really doing
is hoping they will be pleased with and approve of us. We are
giving for our own needs, not for theirs. We are hoping they will
love and accept us, we hope they will not trigger our pain, make us
feel unworthy or bad.

In fact, taking care of everybody except ourselves is an addiction,
another way to keep our emotional demons at bay.

CHAPTER 9

♦ ♦ ♦ ♦ ♦

Addictions:
Silencing the Therapist Within™

The toad that wanted to avoid the rain, fell into the water
Bayansi Proverb

If emotional turmoil is the result of keeping our uncomfortable
feelings inside, addictions, in the broad sense, are all the things
we do to make sure they stay there. *Addictions are what we do
to suppress emotional distress when we don't know any other way
to deal with it.*

Addictions are our attempt to outwit nature, a way to keep feelings
that *want* to come out from coming out. It's as if, having
accidentally ingested poison, we do everything in our power to
thwart the body's natural impulse to get rid of it. Addictions are a
fight between what *we* want—to keep from feeling distress, and
what *nature* wants—to get rid of the pain. They are a battle

between my will (the neocortex) and thy will (the amygdala). It is a battle that nature is destined, at least in the long run, to win.

Addictions are a way of coping, sometimes passed down from generation to generation, that we learned explicitly or implicitly from our parents, our friends, and our culture. We are generally so accustomed to a particular addiction that the behavior commonly kicks in before we are consciously aware of any emotional discomfort.

Whether or not an activity or substance qualifies as an addiction depends not on its character but on how you feel if you stop. Work, for example, is usually a perfectly healthy activity. But it can be an addiction for those who have difficulty relaxing, are often tense and moody when they have a day off, or are comfortable only when engaged in an interesting project. Former President Clinton was reported to be so edgy when on vacation that his aides drew straws to see who the unlucky person to accompany him to Martha's Vineyard would be.

> There is more to life than increasing its speed.
> —Gandhi

Similarly, moderate exercise is physically and psychologically beneficial, but if Sam is desolate whenever he has an injury or Joanne trains to the point where her period stops though she wants to conceive, it is an addiction. The occasional drink doesn't qualify, but if it is habitually used to feel better, it does.

> *One of the ways that I used was extreme physical exercise, especially when I was feeling anxious. I mean extreme. Just going to the gym for hours and hours and hours till I was so exhausted I didn't feel anything. It would be like a numbing. Or I would get intensely involved in some sort of mission, or some sort of pet project, I would make up for myself. Or helping some friend, trying to fix their problems, trying to fix everyone else's problems instead of*

looking at my own. Or projecting them on others. That was another thing I would do. Like thinking that the other person was the one that had the fear instead of me. And I would look down on them, judge them, when it was me that was afraid. A lot of controlling, a lot of fixing other people's problems.

Addictions are as creative as the people who come up with them. They include substances and activities that we generally associate with dulling or overwhelming uncomfortable sensations—so called traditional addictions. But they also include less recognized behaviors such as obsessive thinking, avoidance, and control, some of which are so common, they are considered "normal." While the categories overlap, most people "specialize" in one type or the other.

As I go through this list, check off those that apply to you. Do you habitually numb your feelings or are you an excitement junkie? Do you control or avoid?

Conventional Addictions

• *Numbing addictions:* are generally preferred by those who suffer from anxiety and feel powerless, often because they don't know where the anxiety is coming from, or how to change their circumstances. Numbing addictions include marijuana, alcohol, food, and mood-altering prescription medication. They can involve endless rounds of solitaire or video games, mesmerizing music or rhythms, excessive television, all of which are hypnotic and soothing in nature. People engaged in numbing behaviors are sometimes accused of being lazy or lacking ambition. Others appear to be depressed, or to not care much about anything. The problem is that by dulling uncomfortable feelings, all sensations are depressed, producing a

> We must see to it that our guardians do not become numb or dulled. If they become mute or debilitated, deaf or drunken, they are of no use to us.
> —*Konrad Stettbacher*

105

flat affect, or lack of discernible emotions. The effect of numbing activities can be summed up in one of the favorite words of unhappy members of the younger generation. "Whatever."

• *Excitement addictions:* are substances or activities that overpower discomfort with stronger, more pleasant feelings. They often involve thrill seeking behavior, "dangerous" sex, pornography, shopping, gambling, fast driving, skydiving or other high-wire activities that pump up adrenaline and drown out subterraneous distress. They include cocaine, methamphetamines, and even deliberate evocation of feelings that one is madly in love, just because it feels good. Those who favor excitement addictions generally feel more power over their lives than those who prefer to numb their feelings. These are often the addiction of choice among people who like to be in charge and in control. Witness the presence of "dangerous sex" in so many different political circles.

> It is an ironic habit of human beings to run faster when we have lost our way.
> —Rollo May

Common but Unconventional Addictions

The next three categories of behavior are not usually considered addictions. Some of them are deemed praiseworthy, others thought of as character defects, a few, taken to extreme even criminal. They may be less obvious than the two previous categories of addictions, and don't have the same stigma that is associated with drunkenness or morbid obesity, for example, but they have exactly the same intent—to prevent emotional distress from surfacing. Remember, the defining characteristic of an addiction is not a particular attribute of the activity or substance. It is not about loving to shop or liking the taste of gin. It is about pushing away discomfort, stopping emotional homeostasis from taking place.

• *Thinking addictions.* Thinking, when feeling would be the healthier choice, is so common in Western culture, it is considered not only normal but even laudable. In times of stress, thinkers escape into intellectual discussions, reading and positive thinking exercises. In extreme discomfort they may be overwhelmed by obsessive thinking and analysis paralysis, carrying on endless discussions with friends and family—or just with themselves.

Thinkers are found in abundance in the professions—the legal, medical, academic, and the political communities. It is the addiction of choice for the psychiatric community. Their most reliable clients are those who are hooked on the kind of long-term therapy that allows them to "talk about" their problems without actually feeling them. Crystal doesn't have a therapist, but she calls her friend Sybil at all hours of the day and night. Sybil duly gives her friend her best advice, but Crystal rarely takes it. Crystal doesn't really want advice. The real purpose of her call is to make sure she stays in the intellect and keep her feelings from surfacing.

> What AA calls stinkin thinkin is analytical, obsessive thinking, the constant attempt to figure things out.
> —Anne Wilson Schaef

Thinkers often have difficulty making decisions. Robert is so caught up in neocortical activity—gathering information about potential professions—that he is having difficulty detaching long enough to allow the amygdala—the value-laden part of the brain—to make the choice. While he thinks he just doesn't have enough information, that he needs to talk to more people, further ponder this choice or that, make more lists and consider the pros and cons of each alternative in more depth, he is really stuck. He can't "feel" the right decision. He can't get to the emotional brain, because he is caught in the thinking brain.

> *I had a lot of trouble with – I would call them obsessive thoughts where I would just think of a problem that I had or something that was troubling me and I would just work it over and over and over in my brain and just go round and round. And the more I thought about it the worse it would*

appear and more the insurmountable it would seem to me. It was just an endless cycle of bad thoughts. The thinking was something where I would just go around and around with a problem. And a lot of times it would happen in the middle of the night, when it was just a torturous experience of waking up with a start in the middle of the night thinking "oh my god," what am I going to do about this, what if this happens, what if that happens, what should I do. What's going to become of me, how can I deal with this, how can I change it. I think it was bad for my health just as well to have those obsessive thoughts.

• *Avoidance addictions.* Those who habitually flee when they are uncomfortable either do it physically—leave the arena of discomfort—or psychologically—the body stays but the brain turns off. Avoiders sometimes have a reputation of being laid back and easy to get along with or irresponsible, but in reality they are afraid of what will happen if they are honest and direct. Typically, avoiders withdraw because they don't feel strong enough to deal with whatever is on the table. Something about the circumstances they are in triggers an old stored memory in which they were a dependent child and the "other" the powerful parent. The ultimate avoidance behavior is suicide.

Some avoiders are passive aggressive. They say "all the right things" and deny feeling hostile, but their behavior doesn't jibe with their words. Jerry and Jane had been dating for a number of months when Jerry called to tell her he was having lunch with one of her favorite artists the following day. When he hung up without inviting her to join them, Jane was stunned. Why, she wondered, did he call her and tell her about the lunch date if he wasn't planning to invite her? When she phoned him back to call him on the behavior, he denied being angry, and neither explained why he hadn't invited

> Technology: The knack of so arranging the world that we don't have to experience it.
> —Max Frisch

her, nor did he extend an invitation. Jerry was angry, all right, but anger was either an unacceptable emotion in his family of origin, or he had been, as a child, afraid of the consequences of saying exactly what he felt.

Avoidance is the addiction of choice for phobics. Phobia's, regardless of their type, are in essence, extreme childhood fear trying to come out. Fear of flying is typically described as fear that the bottom will fall out or that the pilots aren't reliable and is commonly experienced by those whose childhood experience was chaotic and unstable. Agoraphobia—panic attacks when in places or situations in which escape may be difficult—is an indication that one may have been trapped as a child, perhaps enduring sexual abuse, beatings from which there was no escape.

Avoidance is the feeling behind defensiveness. If you make a comment that makes me uncomfortable and I immediately strike back with denial instead of stopping to consider your observation, I am avoiding an uncomfortable feeling that you triggered.

Under some circumstances, anger can even be considered an avoidance addiction. Scratch the surface of anger and you will generally find extreme fear, sadness, and pain that the angry person doesn't want to feel. Kitty's left-wing family was devastated during the McCarthy era. Throughout her childhood her father, feeling very much the victim openly expressed his fury with what he perceived to be an all-powerful government. When Kitty attended a *Therapist Within*™ seminar, she too was angry. She had already tried to get her rage out by punching pillows and kicking concrete posts, but even weeks of daily explosions didn't help. The fury did not cease until she was able to reach down past the anger to the fear and panic she had felt as a child when she interpreted her situation as one whose parents were so weak, they could not protect her from outside forces.

Avoiders isolate themselves from events or people they fear may evoke emotional distress. Marshall Applewhite created a cult and had himself castrated to eliminate sexual temptations. The Taliban does it by confining women to the home so that the men won't be tempted by "unacceptable sensations." Sally, 38, hasn't dated in more than a dozen years because trying to put together a relationship was too painful. Roger "turns off" and doesn't listen to his wife when she wants to talk because he "doesn't want to hear it" and agrees to discuss an issue at a later date, but conveniently "forgets." Paula lets the bills pile up because just thinking about opening them fills her with anxiety. Tom avoids telling his girlfriend why he wants to break up with her and just "fades away." Georgia claims that when her husband left her for another woman, it was a complete surprise. Kevin tells his wife he is working late, when, in truth, he is having an affair.

> *One of the problems I had was avoiding problems and feelings. It was very difficult for me to express the feelings I had and therefore, the way I dealt with that was avoiding. This has caused me trouble in my business and professional life as well in dealing with one particularly difficult client. I was so emotionally distraught over the situation, and I couldn't find the right way to tell her what the problem was and what was bothering me. So my way of dealing with that was to avoid it and try to be the perfect consultant and do perfect work, but still, I felt almost sick whenever it was time to talk with this client and certainly I was not at all comfortable in expressing my feelings with her.*

• *Control addictions.* Controllers avoid distress either by exercising internal willpower, or by manipulating the external environment and the people in it so that the "old stuff" won't be

> Let there be no doubt: as long as you continue to blame others instead of assuming your responsibilities, you will make no meaningful and enduring change for the better.
> —*Gary Ryan Blair*

triggered in the first place. They include internal and external efforts to exercise power over one's emotions.

Control behaviors that are focused *internally* include obsessive compulsive disorder (OCD), anorexia, and cutting. OCD— repeating a behavior like checking to see if the doors are locked or washing one's hands to the point where they are raw—are attempts to push down a potential panic attack. Anorexia reflects a desire to present a perfect and proper face to the public (rather than one's internal reality). Cutting which typically occurs when emotional behavior is unacceptable, is an attempt to get one's feelings out physically and literally by creating an opening in the body instead of expelling it naturally. Princess Diana, after years in an undemonstrative royal family, became a cutter.

Control directed *externally* involves other people and includes lying, manipulation, blame, nagging, violence, stalking, and "spin" among other things. Behind attempts to control is the mistaken belief that if the other person changes, if I can shape the environment differently, *I won't hurt*. It is mistaken, of course, because regardless of the degree of success one has in controlling outside events, the "old stuff" is still there, waiting in the amygdala to be triggered by some other stimulus. The ultimate control behavior is murder.

Because the environment is so laden with events and people that can trigger painful emotional memories, control is a lifetime task. Unlike avoiders, the controller spends an enormous amount of energy "fighting" to make the

> I believed in the power of my own will. Whenever the abuse came into my mind, I would say 'I'm not going to think about this.' It was my way to fight back. Denial became synonymous with survival. How could it hurt me if I didn't think about it?
> —*Richard Berendzen*

environment into what they think it should be—and what it should be, they think, is whatever doesn't trigger their pain.

Controllers can be sweetly manipulative or rigid and hostile in their attempts to protect themselves from what they sincerely believe is the source of their emotional distress. Rochelle, a guest on a recent Oprah show was the penultimate "controlling wife." She kept a notebook of instructions for her husband John: don't leave the table before I do, fold my jeans in thirds, fold your own in half, push the chair all the way in, even precise instructions on how to brush his teeth before bed. Of particular concern is that her husband do nothing that she might interpret as disrespect. But what Rochelle is really asking of John is that he never trigger any of the thousands of childhood memories of disrespect she suffered at the hands of her controlling father.

To some controllers, especially thinker types, life is a chess game. They are uncomfortable just letting life flow and base their behavior not so much on what they feel as on what they want to happen. They don't buy into the idea that if one is courageous, tells the truth and lives with integrity, the best will come automatically. When Tabatha's colleague Bret flew to California to nail down some consulting jobs—and to see a woman he was interested in— Tabatha, who was interested in Bret herself, was careful to stay closely in touch with him. On the afternoons of the nights he was free, she called with updates on the office and emergency reports that "had to be written" that evening. The day before he and his friend were to spend a long weekend together, she summoned him home for an urgent meeting that was mysteriously postponed as soon as he landed.

Because of the interdependency involved, the feelings a spouse or lover triggers are the closest one gets to childhood anger and fears. At the extreme, the attempt to avoid these triggers erupts into spousal abuse and violence. Greg made a positive comment about someone of the opposite sex and his wife flew into an angry tirade and demanded that he never make such comments again. Behind the tirade were memories of being abandoned. Ann made an off hand remark that so enraged Bob that he hit her. Behind the anger was the constant stinging criticism of his parents.

The basis of the need to control is fear: fear of the feelings that are starting to come up, fear that it will all "fall apart," fear that you will not get what you need in life. This feeling is most often associated with stored childhood experiences of loss and abandonment, criticism and rejection, some of the most threatening experiences for a child.

> *David was an alcoholic and on various medications. He liked to go out and party a lot and I felt like I was the one who had to be forced to go out with him just to make sure that he would be OK. I had to be in control, and I couldn't possibly be relaxed. . . .*

> *I would make things very difficult for him. I wouldn't allow him to drive the cars, I turned down invitations, I was very controlling, kept things neat and orderly, so he would try to focus himself on getting well, which did not work. And in trying to be a controlling person, all I was doing was making him that much more angry. His response was to drink more, take more pills, get number, and yet he would point the finger at me, that I was the one at fault, which would in turn, made me an even more controlling person. Because I felt I was doing something wrong. Why isn't he listening to me, I wondered?*

> *It really brought back memories of something I had not remembered for a long time. That my mother was addicted to Valium and also drank quite heavily. She was on approximately four Valiums per day and also had two drinks upon arriving home every single day. And that forced my mother into a nervous breakdown, and that is what brought that fear. Why couldn't I make it better?*

The Power of Mother Nature

Mother Nature is a powerful parent. The more we challenge her, the stronger she grows. As we ignore our body's pain and resist its attempts to make us well, as we turn to addictions with increasing frequency, full-blown phobias emerge from anxiety, depression from sadness, terror from fear. We may have the sensation that we are going to "blow up" but are torn between the urge to expel the pain and the fear of letting go.

The addictive person unwittingly chooses a slow crescendo of agony rather than the sharp pain of an incision that would remove the original "emotional tumor" and make him well. But in the long run, addictions don't work. They are like putting a cap on an active volcano. The pressure builds, only to explode when we least expect it.

> When one door of happiness closes, another opens: but often we look so long at the closed door that we do not see the one which has opened for us.
> —Helen Keller

Kip Kinkel, an awkward dyslexic in a family of overachieving intellectual athletes, didn't have an acceptable way to expel his rage at not being able to live up to, what was for him, an impossible external standard. His parents didn't believe in violence—as a child even 'Bugs Bunny' cartoons were banned from the household. "He was not allowed to have little soldiers or any kind of toy that had any kind of violent anything," comments his older sister, Kristin. "Violence in our house was a huge no-no."

What does a child who is furious—even with himself—do with his feelings if it is not OK to express them? Kip's mother took him to see a psychologist, and asked Dr. Hicks to help Kip "manage his anger without resorting to explosives." What this all too often means is to help someone fix his feelings with his thoughts, to talk about feelings rather than feel them, to decide that one's feelings are "wrong," and force them further underground, to evaluate the "correctness" of feelings rather than just letting them out.

As we know, Kip Kinkel's rage erupted into the murder of four people.

The success of addictions is temporary. The more we try to ignore the impulse to expel our pain, the stronger it gets. If we don't pay attention when the pain is mild, we will have to when it is severe.

> *Richard splashed cold water on his face and forced the explosion that occurred in his parents' bedroom back underground. Within months he was overwhelmed with a powerful compulsion to make strange phone calls to child-care workers, asking them about their sexual beliefs. He was soon caught.*

Nature will have her way with us in the end because of the last powerful principle of the Therapist Within™:

We attract that which triggers old pain.

From Turmoil to Tranquility

CHAPTER 10

♦ ♦ ♦ ♦ ♦

Life Crises:
Attracting That Which Triggers Old Pain

The Beauty of Mother Nature is her ability to make complex things appear simple. *Louis E. Samuels, M.D.*

It was a strange family, according to neighbors. And over the previous twelve years, they had attempted to "grow" an even a stranger house. What was originally a nondescript 1400-square-foot ranch home was now a partially completed, three-story 8500-square-foot castle complete with multiple turrets, unfinished wiring, and staircases to nowhere right in the midst of conservative, conformity-minded white-bread Orange County, California. After years of wrangling, the city council declared the home a death trap. They had had enough. As of midnight, the Ganishes would move out and the wrecking ball would move in.

The threat of eviction capped a decade long battle between the Ganishs, their neighbors, and the city of Irvine. There had been far too many skirmishes to count. Multiple violations of building codes, criminal complaints, court hearings, guilty misdemeanor pleas, fines, ultimatums, broken deals, missed deadlines, and finally a police raid. What they found in the end, amongst the starlings living in the rafters and the debris on the floor, were more than 100 fire, health, and safety hazards.

What Haym Ganish experienced during the raid was quite unexpected. They were flashbacks to his childhood and the day Nazi soldiers nearly abducted him and his family.

Why did the Ganishs put themselves in this position? It isn't as if they had no warning. In fact, six months before the wrecking ball was to be unleashed, a deal was made preventing the city from demolishing the house unless Ganish missed a construction deadline. He missed the very first one.

Hyam Ganish is not stupid. And he isn't crazy. His experience demonstrates an immutable law of the *Therapist Within™*: We *attract that which triggers old pain.* We attract people and events that evoke the same traumatic feeling that we stored so many years ago. The principle operates no matter what we do and no matter what we want.

Most life crises are not random or accidental. We don't attract dysfunctional relationships because we are sick, insecure, or have a bad self-image. It isn't that we don't love ourselves or have learned to behave this way from our parents. It is not because we are worthy or unworthy, attractive or unattractive. Life crises and painful relationships are last ditch attempts by the *Therapist Within™* to rid us of poisonous feelings, when we have

> You can't always get what you want. But if you try sometimes, you just might find you get what you need.
> —Mick Jagger

resisted previous signals to do so. They are an attempt to make us well and emotionally whole.

By attracting the experiences and people that trigger old pain, we have an opportunity to get rid of the pain of the past, completely and permanently. Crises give us a doorway to the past. It is healthy. It is normal. It is a miracle. It is not the crisis that is the problem, it is how we respond to it.

What Are Life Crises?

The definition of life crises is broad. Relationships are the primary source of them, especially Velcro relationships (you know, those instantaneous connections that are so emotionally powerful and even sometimes obsessive). But life crises includes other problems as well, problems such as

> When it is dark enough, you can see the stars.
> —*Charles A. Beard*

- Financial difficulties and bankruptcy
- Job and career problems
- Legal problems
- Many of our physical problems, weight difficulties and some illnesses
- Problems with children, in-laws, friends.

What is doesn't include are those rare random events such as
- Drive by shootings
- Physical handicaps
- Random crime
- Eventual illness and death
- Earthquakes and other "natural disasters"

The life crises that we attract can be simple or complex, and are beyond our conscious control, but they have one thing in common: They trigger our old emotional "stuff," and as soon as they do – and we get rid of it - we no longer attract them.

Life crises are a symptom of an advanced emotional infection

Life crises tell you nothing about your self-worth, your intelligence, your character. But they do say something about your ability to push subtle signals aside.

Mother Nature is a gentle teacher. She first tosses a number of pebbles, then rocks, minor crises, all opportunities to pay attention to and get rid of the original pain, before dislodging a boulder. Just as in physical illness, the severity of the crisis is associated with how long and how forcefully we have ignored our symptoms.

The initial symptoms of an emotional infection are mild and internal, a sniggling little feeling perhaps of anxiety or sadness, the first indication of an old feeling that wants to come out. If, instead of allowing the feeling to emerge, we ignore it, secondary symptoms – negative thoughts, perhaps – will begin to appear. If we continue to push these feelings down with positive thinking, affirmations, and the

> Sweet are the uses of adversity
> Which, like the toad, ugly and venomous
> Wears yet a precious jewel on his head.
> —*William Shakespeare*

like, we will automatically and unconsciously begin to behave in ways that sometimes appear to be "dysfunctional." Perhaps we will chose a difficult relationship despite the fact that there are warning bells, or take a job with a boss who, after a few months on the job, triggers memories of your unavailable father. Or, perhaps we avoid opening the bills and facing financial dilemmas. In the end, if we continue to push the feelings aside, in the mistaken notion that if we don't feel them, they don't exist, we will attract life crises – the mate who suddenly leaves, the job that disappears, the bill collector who shows up at our door. Nature will act in an ever-increasing crescendo until we pay attention to her message and do what she wants. Often, such crises balloon into magical thinking or flights from reality.

*I've had lots of imagined crises, and actually
hallucinations or out of body projections. See ghosts, even,
and think that somebody was trying to kill me. Really crazy
stuff. Think the house was haunted. It's kind of
embarrassing really, but I would just have all of these
imagined fears that I think I actually projected out of
myself and would manifest into thinking someone could
read my mind, or was invading my privacy, that I was
under control and trapped. And all of these came to a head
several times, different times throughout this year. I
remember once when I was laying in bed and this happened
about 7 months ago, and all of a sudden I just got this very
strong urge to just get out, to just run, run, run, keep
driving in my car and just run away.*

*I remember once being so frightened of flying that I
actually believed that my thoughts could bring a plane
down. I mean, I knew logically that it probably couldn't
happen, but I was terrified that it would.*

The crises we attract are based on subjective feelings, not objective facts.

We attract those things that remind us of the same *feelings* as the
ones we originally stored. The objective facts of the event or
person may be very different, but the feeling generated is the same.
Jack, a seminar participant told us that he had deliberately chosen
very different types of women as his last two girlfriends. One was
short, the other tall, one outgoing, the other shy, one a stockbroker,
the other a librarian. Both of them, however, made him feel as if
he couldn't rely on them, an old feeling, Jack admitted. They both
generated in him the same *feeling*. When thinking about the kind
of crises you attract, the kind of people, etc., go into the bodily
sensations, the feelings you have about them. You will often find a
common thread that weaves through your life.

Whether or not we attract these crises is not under our conscious control

The only way to be sure to avoid similar crises is by eliminating the stored feeling that engenders it. Like all functions of the amygdala, attracting and being attracted to that which triggers old pain involves intuition and the ability to perceive complex patterns that are not apparent to the linear, rational neocortex. Although Jack in the previous example used his rational mind to choose someone he believed was very different from his first girlfriend, he was attracted to and selected as his second girlfriend, a woman who turned out to have the same character traits as the first. We can't know how this happens any more than we can know how nature knows where to send our white blood cells or which ones to send to the site of an infection.

A crisis can be simple or complex, direct or circuitous.

But how could Haym Ganish have known what was to befall him? His neocortex, his linear, conscious mind couldn't have known. But his amygdala, the instinctive and intuitive mind, the genius of Mother Nature did.

Without recognizing the connection, Ganish, regarding his present conflict with Orange County, talks of harassment and police brutality, of a government that tries to take anything away from anybody, of complex government plots and politicians who "run like dogs"

How does this phenomenon work? In a complex universe it may not be possible to ever know exactly *how* we attract that which triggers old pain any more than it is to know how, if we are truly in touch with our body's messages, we know what to eat. But the phenomenon is probably related to what quantum physics calls non-locality – or the butterfly effect -

> A good fortune may forbode a bad luck, which may in turn disguise a good fortune.
> —*Chinese Proverb*

the mysterious ability of particles to affect other particles, no matter how distant in time and space.

Suffice it to say, Mother Nature wants first and foremost for us to be healthy and whole, and, because none of the functions of the amygdala are under our direct control, the principle operates no matter what we do, how we think, and regardless of what we want.

> *For some reason, I always attracted the kind of guy that criticized me, walked out and abandoned me, and was totally unreliable. Each one of them was so like my dad. Some were even alcoholics like he was. I don't know what it is about them. When I meet a truly nice guy, I am just not attracted to them.*

> *My mother was so smothering and controlling. I swore I would never marry somebody like her and here I am, married to a woman who is afraid to let me out of her sight, somebody who nags me about everything.*

> *My life as a child was so chaotic. We never lived anywhere for long, my dad was always losing jobs, and then he walked out on us. I always wanted security, but I don't seem to have the ability to get it for myself. I've had lots of jobs; I'm being laid off, constantly, nothing seems to last long.*

Fifth, life crises and dysfunctional relationships are usually mutual

They usually serve the growth and healing needs of both parties equally. Someone who experienced severe financial difficulty when they were young may attract a partner who develops a gambling problem or shopping compulsion. Persons who have experienced fear of abandonment in their childhood, often attract a mate who fears suffocation and is unfaithful. The couple will trigger each other's stuffed feelings in a dance that can be beneficial to both of them *if* they know how to use the turmoil to erase old pain. Again, we may never know how this happens, but when we look closely at relationships, it is clear that it does.

> You can complain because roses have thorns,
> or you can rejoice because thorns have roses.
> —ZIGGY

The other day, a client asked me how she could get her husband to be more polite with her. She reacted with anger each time he was rude, and was thinking that his rudeness was the problem. I reminded her that his rudeness was simply triggering an old emotional memory – in this case, of her father's rude behavior and that when she erased the old memory, she would probably react to her husband's rudeness with indifference or even humor.

What kind of crises do you have? What kind of relationships have you chosen? What kind has walked into your life? Who are you attracted to and who is attracted to you? What feelings do they trigger? Do these feelings remind you – feel like – anything else in your distant past?

One last comment. Because it is impossible to know exactly who the other person is in any troubled relationship until our old pain has been erased, it is important not to jump to conclusions. For example, Sally, whose childhood was chaotic and insecure, fears abandonment. Jerry, her husband is attracted to other women. Is Jerry an irresponsible man who does not take his commitments seriously? Or, is his attraction (but not behavior) a result of the constant nagging and accusations of infidelity he has endured during his 10 year

> Even from a dark night, songs of beauty can be born
> —Maryanne Radmacher-Hershey

marriage to Sally? Until Sally gets rid of the original pain, and stops nagging him, there is no way to tell.

Is Penny's husband being rude as she contends, or is he simply direct and straightforward as he believes? When Penny gets rid of the original pain of feeling unvalued, she will know.

George is defensive and quick to believe that others, particularly his girlfriends are critical. But after he erases the memories of his tumultuous childhood and critical parents, he may no longer interpret the slightest comment as a criticism. He will interpret his relationships in a whole new light. Once the "old stuff" is erased, he will be able to determine quite objectively if they are critical or not.

Unfortunately, however, we all too often respond to life crises – with our addictions – thinking, avoiding, controlling, drinking, eating, blaming. Such a response is not only futile, it creates greater crises as nature tries to break through our resistance and make us whole. What we need to do is to excavate the emotional infection and get rid of it once and for all. We need to have an emotional orgasm and *just let go*.

PART III
The Process

How to Have
an Emotional Orgasm
. . . and Just Let Go

Six Steps to Emotional Freedom

PART III

Today

Step 1: Make the Decision

Step 2: Awaken Your Emotional Brain

Step 3: Surface Your Stuff

Step 4: Relinquish Control

Step 5: Restore the Mind/Body Connection

Step 6: Rehearse

The Big Picture

Today

◆ ◆ ◆ ◆ ◆

A s I look back on that explosive moment in Russia, it is as a different person. The pain is gone, the struggle, the angst. There are no more terrors or panic attacks, no anxiety or fear. I sleep at night. Even the life crises have disappeared. It is as if someone had thrown a thousand puzzle fragments into the air and they had landed in one piece. The experience in Russia had produced a psychological and spiritual transformation so deep and profound that, even now, it leaves me breathless.

It was so simple, so easy, intrinsic and innate. Why hadn't I gotten it before? What had I missed? Over the previous 20 years I had devoured thousands of pop psych books, tuned into hundreds of trendy talk shows, and sought help from scores of reputable therapists. But none of it had helped. At least not for long.

"Before Russia," had anyone described the river of life as a smoothly flowing stream while I was struggling in the rapids I would have thought he was from Mars. If anyone had encouraged me to let go of whatever branch I was clinging to, or told me that I would be safe as I rode over the falls to the jagged rocks below, I would have thought she was delusional. If anyone had suggested to me that there even *was* a river of life, I would have dismissed him as a New Age nitwit. I had never floated in the gentle stream of life. It was a concept that did not compute.

The idea of it was like trying to describe the color of the sky to the blind or the sound of Mozart to the deaf.

But now, there was a way out, a way to heal. It had been in front of me always. It was a separate source of information, a source as powerful as words, perhaps more so. The directions had been in my body's sensations all along. It was available, is available to everyone at all times.

CHAPTER 11

♦ ♦ ♦ ♦ ♦

Step 1: Make the Decision
One Giant Leap

The moment one definitely commits oneself, then providence moves too. All sorts of wonderful things occur to help one that would never otherwise have occurred. A whole stream of events issues from the decision, raising on one's favor all manner of unforeseen incidents and meetings and material assistance which no man could have dreamed would come his way. Whatever you can do or dream, you can begin it. Boldness has genius, power, and magic in it. Begin it now. *Goethe*

Supposing I were to tell you that there is only one thing you need to do to eliminate emotional distress, relationship horrors, life crises and even many illnesses? One tiny little thing that your body wants to do anyway. One tiny little thing that is nature's way of erasing old trauma? That if you do this one thing, you won't have to think about your issues anymore. You won't have to read any more self-help books, talk about your problems, get therapy, or take medication?

What if I were to tell you that if you do this one thing, emotional turmoil, relationship difficulties, and life crises would automatically evaporate? That you would, without even thinking about it, set boundaries, speak the truth, attract and be attracted to healthy people, raise happy children, and be joyful and serene? That you could make decisions faster, be assertive at the right moments, be fully intuitive?

And what if I were to tell you that the one thing you need to do is to *express the distress you stored as a child, exactly the way you were supposed to express it when the original trauma occurred. That you wouldn't need to remember the details of the original incident, that you wouldn't need to express the feelings to anyone at all but yourself, but that you would need to express them not with words, but with actions such as anger and tears?*

And what if I told you that you don't need to do this very often, and that you only need to do it when you are in emotional turmoil? That if you do this, the actual physical memory will disappear from the amygdala forever.

Would you say I was crazy? Would you have a difficult time believing that it could be so easy? Listen to some of those who have done it.

> *When I took the class I found it almost too simple. Some of those questions I had were if it were so simple, why didn't I think of it myself? I'd been through years of therapy, very expensive therapy, and I found that the system to be a very simple, matter of fact, practical, way to get rid of my stuff, and when I did it, I felt released. It's gone. It was easy. And I have no fear. I have forgotten so much the things that had bothered me through a very simple process. I'm a changed person.*

My feelings of anxiety and depression were lifted within probably a couple of days. I just didn't have that feeling that had been a part of my life for such long time. I went through this class several months ago, and things have evened out in my life. I've been working on solutions to them and the solutions come to me more easily than they had. They seem to present themselves in a way that they didn't before.

What a week this has been! I have been releasing on a non-stop basis, and my husband is releasing also. I breathe so much better than I ever have, it seems to be a deeper more satisfying breath. I also noticed that things that irritate me come up quicker than before, but instead of yelling at the person that supposedly "caused me to get angry", I quickly internalize the situation and feel it to the max, then release it.

My husband said the release feels exactly like the big "O". Our home is much more peaceful our relationship is improving every day. It was never a bad relationship, but now it is feeling like it did when we first fell in love. April 25th is our 21 wedding anniversary, I could not think of a better gift, than what we've received from this program.

It didn't take too long, maybe about 20 minutes, I'm not sure, and I ended up after that feeling cleaner, more secure, less afraid. It was such a different feeling. Everything looked clearer, even my vision changed from this cloudy red stuff, to like ah, wow, something had lifted off of me. I really don't have any words to describe it. I really don't understand it still. But the main point is that I feel a lot better now, and I feel like something was lifted so that in that sense, whatever happened was important, it was pertinent, and I don't necessarily have to understand it. The main point is I feel better.

Deciding to Feel

The idea that it is difficult to get emotionally healthy is a myth, perpetuated by the idea that we must control our emotions with rational thoughts. *That* is work! Letting go is actually far less work than trying to hang on.

> It takes a tremendous amount of emotional and physical energy to hold down your feelings. Living becomes a struggle to stay in control.
> —*John Gray*

But making the absolute, irrevocable decision to change your emotional life takes energy . . . and courage . . . and honesty. Making the commitment is the critical first step to emotional freedom, and it can be challenging to gather enough energy to do so for a number of reasons.

♦ When your habit is to use so much of your energy to keep your feelings from overwhelming you, you must make a clear decision to do the opposite

♦ If you are not in touch with your physical/emotional feelings you may be suffering from chronic illnesses, (often undetected), poor diets, inadequate sleep and low energy levels

> Following the Noble Path is like entering a dark room with a light in the hand; the darkness will all be cleared away and the room will be filled with light.
> —*Buddah*

♦ Stopping the habit of escaping to your addictions, your thoughts, or trying to control others takes focus and determination

Don't take my word for the importance of this decision. What does your gut say about the choice of feeling or suppressing feeling? Which do you sense is the right decision for your long-term peace of mind? Making the decision to change is the key. The rest is downhill.

Imagining the Future

Are you ready to make that commitment? Can you imagine a life without emotional upheavals, crises, distress? How would your work change? Your significant relationships? What kinds of excitement could you substitute for your life crises? Do you want to go river-rafting? Have lunch in a Paris bistro? Climb the Himalayas? Visit Machu Pichu? Go sky diving? Take your kids or grandkids on a hike?

If you were rid of your anxiety, anger and sadness, what would you be doing with your life, instead of what you are doing now? What could you accomplish if the energy you are using to keep your feelings in check were freed? What if you could sleep peacefully through the night? If you stopped turning your problems over and over in your mind. How could you contribute to the community? To your family? To yourself?

Picture yourself in healthy, supportive relationships without crises and fights. Imagine attracting and being attracted to friends and lovers who were caring, demonstrative, responsible, and loving. Imagine getting your excitement from doing fun things with those you love instead of fighting with them.

> Courage is the price that life exacts for granting peace. The soul that knows it not, knows no release from little things.
> —*Amelia Earhart*

Take a few minutes right now and every day both when you awaken and when you snuggle down for the night to picture your life anxiety-free. See yourself doing all the things you are unable to do today. Picture yourself with friends and family, talking, laughing, enjoying a crisis-free day, week, month, and year. Make the scene as real as possible.

Understanding the Goal

The goal of the Six Steps to Serenity is to dissolve old emotional memories by *turning up the volume of your internal world*, Mother

135

Nature's voice, and *turning down the volume of the external world.*
Instead of concentrating on the behavior of others, you will begin
to deliberately pay attention to the events taking place inside your
body. You will move your focus from what others are doing to
what you are feeling – not thinking! – *about* what they are doing.
In other words, you will focus on *what stored feelings of yours* are
being triggered by others' behavior. By following all six steps,
you will learn how to allow these feelings to come to the surface
and dissolve.

Jane came to me with a typical problem. Her boyfriend was a flirt,
and worse, he was obvious about it. At first, she framed the
problem with an external orientation:

> *When I walk down the street with my boyfriend, Hank ogles*
> *all the pretty girls. This is so disturbing to me. I have*
> *talked to him until I am blue in the face and he still does it.*
> *Sometimes I just want to hit him, or start ogling guys to get*
> *back at him. I just want him to stop.*

After some discussion, Jane was able to turn her focus into an
internal orientation which allowed her to access her feelings of
insecurity and fear.

> *When I walk down the street with my boyfriend, he ogles all*
> *the pretty girls. This puts my stomach in a knot. I have an*
> *incredible feeling of fear. As if I am not pretty enough for*
> *him and he is going to leave me. I have talked to him about*
> *it and he still doesn't stop. I feel so disrespected, like my*
> *feelings don't count. It reminds me of when I was a little*
> *girl and my father left us. I begged him and begged him to*
> *stay, and he still left.[3]*

---

[3] *I am not suggesting, in this example, that Hank's behavior is respectful. But when Jane dissolves
the old memories of her father, she will automatically behave in such a way that either Hank will
stop his obnoxious behavior or Jane will leave him.*

At first this may take conscious effort. You have been oriented outward and trying to "figure out your issues" intellectually for years – asking the "why do I feel this way?" question instead of "what do I feel?" You have kept your feelings at bay for a long time by suppressing them. These are well-ingrained habits. But as the "old stuff" dissolves and disappears, focusing on your own internal guidance system will become automatic. After all, it is the way Mother Nature designed you.

Medication

It is impossible to completely re-orient from the external world to your inner core if you can't feel completely and fully. All substances that dull or heighten sensation stop you from perceiving what is really going on in your body.

If you are presently taking psychotropic medications, ***do not stop them cold turkey***. Despite what you may believe, many of these medications are highly habit forming. Though pharmaceutical companies claim that their drug will increase a particular neurotransmitter, it often does the opposite. The body, in response to many of these medications, slows its production of the neurotransmitter creating the need for more of the drug. When you try to discontinue the pills, it takes some time before the body is able "crank up" its own production.

> Psychotropic medications can only take the edge off of the illness, not erase past traumas or resolve surrounding issues.
> —*Clinical Psychiatry News*

In one eye-opening on-line article a doctor advises consumers of Xanax how to "come off" this supposedly non-addictive drug without incurring side-effects. The advice is to decrease dosage by .25 milligrams every two weeks, giving the body an opportunity to resume making the neurotransmitter. If a patient is taking 6mg a day, this gradual reduction will take a total of 48 weeks!

But the problem with medication is not simply biological. Some significant broad-based and long-term studies of systematic desensitization and other therapies that advocate reliving old emotional memories, have shown that this kind of therapy *with medication* may be less effective – produce *more* relapses in the long run – than therapy without it.

♦ A 1986 study: depressed patients received nine months of treatment with psychotherapy or antidepressant medication and were evaluated every six months for two years. At the end of two years, only 23% of the patients treated with psychotherapy had relapsed, but 78% of those treated with only medication saw their depression return.

♦ A National Institute of Mental Health study in the 80s: 200 patients received therapy or prescription drugs for depression. At the end of 16 weeks, two-thirds of the patients had responded to the treatment equally. When they were evaluated two years later, however, 50% of those treated with medication had become depressed again compared with 35% of those treated with therapy.

♦ A Scotland study: patients were assessed every six months for two years – by the end of 2 years, 78% of those who had received drugs *only* had relapsed, 23% of those who had therapy *only* had relapsed; those who had gotten both had a relapse rate of 21%, and insignificant difference.

♦ A British study in 1993 on Xanax: patients treated "improved," but only while they remained on the drug. After withdrawal, the effect disappeared on every measure. On a number of measures of anxiety, patients were actually worse off than those who had received a placebo.

Most of the time, these medications are a bad idea. They upset the balance of neurotransmitters in the entire body and often result in your body being *less* capable of producing the amount you need. These medications should be used primarily on an emergency, short-term basis. If you would like to learn more, you can find reliable information from Dr. Peter Breggin, prominent psychiatrist and expert on psychotropic drugs by reading his books, or checking out his extensive web site, www.breggin.com.

To come off psychotropic drugs see your doctor. Make sure the program of discontinuation is gradual and gives your body a chance to recover its ability to make the neurotransmitters you need. Otherwise, you may incorrectly conclude that you do indeed have a chemical imbalance.

In the meantime, you can continue with the steps of this program. It will help you change your focus and prepare you for the day you are drug-free. Just know that as long as you are on medication, while you may appear to be getting significant relief from you anxiety, it will be short-lived. You will not be able to make significant long-term progress until the medication wears off.

Self-Help versus Therapy

So, should you go it alone, join a self-help group, get a therapist or rely on friends to help you make this change? It depends on you. Some people find it easy to access their feelings when they are alone and hard to go into their emotions when other people are present. They prefer self-help

Self-help: You are a great candidate for self-help if you are

- ♦ self-directed and disciplined.

- ♦ sick and tired of feeling sick and tired i. e. you are ready to give up and let Mother Nature do her job.

- ♦ either not on psychotropic medications or have been on them for a short period of time.

- ♦ blessed to have supportive family or friends who encourage you to express feelings.

- ♦ easily able to cry

If you have access to a 12-step program, so much the better. Though they will not "cure" you, they are a wonderful support system for those going through self-therapy. If you decide to join one of these groups, watch for members who are actually feeling their old stored memories and those who use the group to avoid feeling them. There will be both types in your group in all likelihood. Make friends with those who are in the first category. They will be your supporters in your journey.

Safety in Numbers: Others, however, find it difficult to go into their feelings unless they feel the safety of other people around them. This can be a supportive friend who is comfortable with the expression of feelings, or a professional, depending on your level of emotional distress. But, in general, you will want to get the help of a professional if

- The trauma is so painful you are too frightened to pursue feeling the "old stuff" by yourself

- You have been diagnosed with manic depression, schizophrenia, or any other psychosis

- You have been on psychotropic drugs for a long period of time

- You don't feel disciplined enough or you are too busy to keep yourself on task

Therapy Revisited: In earlier chapters I mentioned that most therapy produces small changes that are short lived and that neither the training and experience of the therapist nor their particular school of thought appears to have anything to do with how effective the therapy will be.

While this statement is accurate, it doesn't go far enough. There *are* many individual cases in which client's lives have been fundamentally and permanently changed by therapy. But it is not the school of thought, training, or length of the therapeutic process that produces these changes.

Instead, I submit, the exceptions to the rule occur in large part when the individual therapist is able (and willing) to focus the clients' attention either deliberately or accidentally on *feeling and re-experiencing* the old stored emotion. Thus, clients of psychoanalysts who encourage emotional catharsis are likely to report more significant improvement than those whose analyst helps them "understand" their issues. Therapists who practice deep-feeling techniques such as systematic desensitization and Eye Movement Desensitization and Reprogramming (EMDR),[4] techniques that require going "into the feeling" – would have significantly better "cure rates" than those who don't. In fact, this is exactly what we find.

So, if professional therapy is the way you want to go, be sure to select a therapist who will help you excavate feelings, not just understand them and make sure they follow through. If you are willing to feel, and your therapist is good, you should be able to make significant progress within a session or two.

A Word about Tears

One last note. Many of you are uncomfortable with showing emotion, especially tears. It can make you feel vulnerable and childish because you are usually shedding tears you were supposed to shed *then;* you are emotionally transported back to the time when you originally experienced these feelings.

I could tell you all the reasons tears are healthy, that, according to Sir Henry Maudsley, "sorrows which find no vent in tears may soon make other organs weep." I could cite studies that tears contain chemicals and proteins that in concentration can cause depression and ulcers. I could tell you that emotional tears have four times as much potassium as plasma, thirty times the amount of

---

[4] *A technique that involves looking at a moving finger while re-living a traumatic memory.*

manganese, and that high concentrations of manganese have also been found in the brains of chronic depressives after their deaths.

I could tell you that in other cultures, crying is not deplored as it is in this one, especially in men. Or that the disdain for tears came in the 20th century with the increasing worship of the rational brain, or that Hippocrates believed in purging and purifying through cathartic tears.

I could tell you that much of the philosophy of joy is based on the ability to cry, that "those who sow in tears reap with shouts of joy." Or that in Luke in the New Testament appears the statement "Blessed are you who weep now, for you shall laugh." And in John – "Your sorrow will be turned into joy." That the Hebrew attitude toward tears is that they are nourishing and sustaining, and that there is an old Yiddish proverb "weeping makes the heart grow lighter."

What I will tell you is this: tears emanating from old stored memories are childhood tears. They are the same tears that you did not shed when you were small and helpless that need to be shed now in order for you not to feel small and helpless as an adult. I will tell you that tears encourage us to shift our focus from our thoughts to our bodies, from our rational minds to our amygdala. I will tell you that if you wish to be a strong, resilient adult human being, you need to cry the tears that you have stifled for so many years.

> Crying, next to love, is perhaps the most healing activity for the heart.
> —Dr. Stephen Sinatra, Cardiologist

The strength and power will come automatically, as the vestiges of childhood are drained away.

CHAPTER 12

♦ ♦ ♦ ♦ ♦

Step 2: Awaken Your Emotional Brain
Getting in Tune with the Amygdala

Miracles seem to rest, not so much upon faces or voices or healing power coming suddenly near to us from afar off, but upon our perceptions being made finer so that for a moment our eyes can see and our ears can hear that which is about us always. Willa Cather

I used to smoke – a whole lot, in fact – four packs a day. I actually smoked in the shower, and even tried to smoke in the ocean and swimming pool (though not very successfully, as you can imagine). There was only one activity (besides sleep) in which I did not smoke. (I will leave that to your imagination.) I needed only one match a day and was resigned to dying by 40 because, as one colleague remarked, "I've never seen you without a cigarette."

Fortunately, an organization called Smokenders™ came to the rescue. One of the key elements of the program was for each participant to keep track of the number of cigarettes smoked each day. A small piece of paper, folded up with mini-pencil inside was placed between the cigarette box and the plastic wrap. Before taking out and lighting the next cigarette, we removed that little piece of paper and checked off another box. There were other simple steps as well, each to make us more mindful of what we were doing. Those who followed the simple directions succeeded in chucking the cigarettes, those that did not, were not.

Record Your Progress

Keeping a daily log such as I kept with Smokenders™ forces an interruption in old habits. In the case of emotional health, that habit is being unaware of your inner sensations. Any small, spiral bound notepad that you can divide into three sections and can easily carry with you will do the trick. Keep it in your pocket or purse, whichever is more convenient, with a small pencil or pen.

The purpose of the log is to increase your attention to three critical elements of your life: *what you love* (who you are), *your triggers* (what causes discomfort), and *how you block the healing process* (your favored addictions).

What You Love:

The sum total of what you love defines who you uniquely are in this world. To be surrounded by the things you care about – the colors, the sounds, the personalities – provides tranquility. But you need to know what those things are, first.

> A hunch is creativity trying to tell you something.
> —*Anonymous*

Jot down any time you get an "ahhhhhh" kind of feeling, as if you were sinking into the plushest club chair. You are truly at home, relaxed, calm and centered. What was it that triggered this sense of serenity? Begin to list all the things you are attracted to: color,

144

sound, music, sensual experiences, type of clothes, look of other people, voices, types of books, leisure time activities, what kinds of conversations do you like to have? What kind of mate do you prefer? What kind of climate suits you? What kind of home? City or town? You needn't have any "reason" for your preferences. They are just . . . *You.*

Go into a paint store and pick up color chips that you are attracted to. Browse the aisles of the local art gallery. What shapes,

> Every Man's story is important, eternal and sacred. That is why every man, as long as he lives and fulfills the will of nature is wonderous and worthy of every consideration.
> —Herman Hesse

colors, sizes, materials are attractive to you? Look at the colors in the paintings. Look at the shadows. What medium is used? How does the artist convey depth in the picture? Take an art appreciation class.

Visit your local bookstore – one that allows you to listen to different types of music. Listen to rock, jazz, blues, gospel, classical. Which ones are you attracted to? Go to a concert. Does the music make you excited? Sad? Angry? How does the music make you feel?

Reflect on what makes you joyful. Get familiar with "home base." Notice when you are feeling good. What makes you feel safe? What kinds of people do you like? What kind of living space? What leisure time activities do you enjoy?

Your Triggers

Keep track of the times you are uncomfortable and distress is raising its ugly head. Note exactly what happened before you begin to feel anxiety. Was it something someone said? A report from the stock market? An event at work? A news report on the state of the world? An event in someone else's life?

Note how you feel in response to the trigger. Are you anxious? Fearful? Sad? Mistrustful? Angry? Go to the next step in describing the feeling. "I feel as if . . . . ." is a good sentence to complete. Try to capture the feeling quickly, before it fades.

- Megan was panic-stricken at the thought of going through a tunnel. She felt it was going to fall in on her, crush and suffocate her

- Bill became livid whenever he felt he was being criticized. He felt that he could never be quite good enough.

- Kristin was afraid of flying. She felt out of control and in danger

- Matthew became upset whenever he was asked to share his food. He felt like he might not get enough.

Your Addictions

Become aware of the times you are fighting your feelings instead of cooperating with them. Notice when you are avoiding a feeling by being dishonest, when you are struggling, when you are afraid. Pay attention to those times you feel defensive and have a closed mind.

- Notice when you are working too hard, struggling to *make* something happen.

- Be aware of the times you are irritable, mildly uncomfortable, feeling antsy with yourself or others.

- Note when you reach for your favorite addictions, when the television is turned on just so you can turn off your feelings, when the drink is meant to drown your anxiety, when avoiding means you are preventing yourself from feeling.

- Watch your feelings – and note when you are beginning to experience anxiety, sadness, or anger.

- Observe your thoughts – when you are first caught in obsessive thinking, or have intrusive thoughts of revenge, or fear.

- Note when you are tempted to lie, control, manipulate or avoid.

- Pay attention to potential life crises when they are in their infancy and let the feelings come up.

Stop reacting outwardly to pain. Just be aware of what you are feeling, and tell yourself that it is old pain trying to come up. Don't try to figure out what it is or

> I always know when they're coming. I get very tense. I get very scared. I get snappy at things that ordinarily wouldn't make me angry.
> —*The Courage to Heal*

where it is coming from. Just feel it and define the feeling. One client relates the process as she struggles with the urge to react.

> *We went to Sedona last weekend and for once had a peaceful good time. Usually, due to the idle time on both ends all kinds of emotions come up and we have big fights about everything he did to me and everything I did to him in the past 21 years. We used the techniques we had learned in your program, had things come up but handled them very well and life is good.*
>
> *Well, that lasted a whole two days. Yesterday my daughter, who graduates from high school May 30th, told me she was probably pregnant.*
>
> *I blew it. I yelled at her for being so irresponsible and for getting pregnant by such a loser. It was an ugly, funny thing. I felt totally justified in how I felt, but today I feel like crap.*
>
> *This is all about me isn't it? All the fears that I had about getting pregnant when I was young came flooding in and pretty much engulfed me emotionally. My mother told me if I got pregnant no man would ever want me, I would be in*

essence "broken." My step-father who tried for years to molest me, once he found out I had a boyfriend said I would be thrown to the streets if ever I came home pregnant.

I made sure I never became pregnant outside of wedlock, so when it happened to my daughter, it happened to me. I had nightmares, I felt sick, dirty, worthless and of course "ruined". I even felt guilty for wishing the problem would go away....

Now, I am on the threshold of seeing things in a new light. The feelings are mine not my daughter's. My concern is for her and the baby. I can see now beyond my fears and just feel concern for her. This baby is already loved beyond life. I will spoil this child rotten with hugs, kisses and unconditional acceptance, and of course my daughter, she is giving this family a priceless gift. Thank you Cindy for your help because of your program I can heal the past instead of just hurting.

What is important in this story is that this client knew that her reaction to her daughter was an addiction: by striking out, she was blaming her "old stuff" on her daughter. And by understanding the process, she was able to go deeply into her own pain, dissolve it and then be supportive.

> The soul's emphasis is always right.
> —Ralph Waldo Emerson

In one section of your log, list each time you either use or are tempted to use an addiction, each time you are caught in obsessive thoughts. Keep track of the times you use the internet, drugs, shopping, gambling or sex to relieve stress, when you call a friend to complain in order to block an emotion. Once a week, search for and highlight the themes that emerge from the log. Are they about anger? Abandonment? Jealousy? Engulfment? Powerlessness?

Sleep and Dreams

If obsessive thoughts are keeping you awake at night, try to switch out of your thoughts and into you body. What are you feeling? Be as specific as possible. If it is fear, exactly what kind of fear does it feel like? Let the feelings surface until you can identify them.

Sleep is a time when Mother Nature tries to resolve whatever emotions were not dissolved during the day – the feelings you suppressed. While you are dreaming, your emotional brain lights up and is as active as it is during your waking hours, while the pre-frontal cortex, the center of reasoning is relatively quiet. For most people, the dreams they have at the beginning of the night are the most disturbing, those at the end of the night more pleasant. This is the mind's way of working through emotional issues, trying to repair the damage, bring to the surface feelings you may have suppressed during the day so that they can become labile (unstable) and dissolve.

If you have disturbing dreams, focus on the feeling you are having when you awaken. Have you ever had that feeling before? Are you dreaming about being chased? Falling? Losing face? Do you feel vulnerable, frightened or angry? Follow the directions in the next two chapters and keep a record in your log. As you learn how to better "process" the feelings during the day, you should see fewer emotionally distressful dreams and more pleasant ones.

Replace Thoughts with Feelings

But how do you *feel*?" It is a question many left-brained people and many men dread. For them, and many of the rest of us, learning about the senses is not like learning French. It's more like learning Chinese. Or Turkish. Because we are so used to using the rational brain to understand our issues and figure out where they are coming from – to think *about* our feelings, the idea that it isn't necessary is a hard concept to accept.

Consider this, however. Do you need to know the exact mechanism by which you recover from a cold? Do you need to know what germ is causing your symptoms, its name, and how it behaves? Do you even need to know much about how your body fights germs? If you had a choice, would you rather know the exact mechanism of a disease, or "sense" what you should do to get rid of it?

You really only need to know what to do when you get certain messages from your body, don't you? You need to know to rest when you feel tired, eat when you are hungry, to drink fluids when you are thirsty, etc. You only need to know how to cooperate with Mother Nature! And that requires paying attention to feelings, not thoughts.

> I asked Berlin to explain. He said 'Well, first stop trying to be the doctor. You've always operated on a cognitive level. We want you to respond on an affective realm and begin to deal with your feelings.' I told him I wasn't sure what he was talking about. 'That's part of your problem,' he replied . . . You're always trying to maintain control. You need to release, let loose . . . Stop intellectualizing. Just let go.'
> —*Richard Berendzen*

Distinguishing between feelings and thoughts *about* feelings requires a paradigm shift, one of those "aha" moments. With a bit of brain-power, a smidgen of practice, and a pinch of patience, however, it will become quite easy to distinguish between them, catch and reorient yourself to sensations. Here are some examples:

George at Work:

George has always had a lot of trouble at work. His latest job in a promising hi-tech firm is turning into the same old story. Harry, his boss, is aggressive with employees, boastful and controlling but is well placed in the company. It is not the first time George has worked for someone like this. He has worked for a string of them. Thanks to the tight job market, he has rarely had to stay in a job more than a year or two. But now that George is married and has a child on the way, he is torn. His mind flits back and forth uncontrollably from one solution to the next. As soon as he thinks he has settled on one solution, he changes his mind. He wants to get rid of the underlying anxiety and anger but can't figure out the difference between his thoughts *about* his feelings and his feelings.

Thoughts about feelings: *My boss is such a jerk, he is going to fire me for sure. It is so unfair. He is such a control freak; I've got to figure out some way to get him fired. He was so unfair to me today. I am sure he is taking credit for all the projects I am doing and not telling anyone that the work is mine. Maybe I should meet with the HR department and ask them to get me transferred to another department.*

Feelings: *I am so scared I am going to be fired. I feel as if I am going to die. It is so bad, my throat is constricted and my nerves are completely on edge. I feel like I am about to go over the edge. I am so angry, my arms feel like they are going to reach out and sock Harry in the nose if he even speaks to me. My muscles are tense and my head is throbbing. I am so frightened that the bottom is going to fall out and I am going to have nothing. Like going into a black hole from which I will never emerge. I am in great danger. I am completely alone. There is no one to save me.*

> If we listened to our intellect, we'd never have a love affair. We'd never have a friendship. We'd never go into business, because we'd be cynical. Well, that's nonsense. You've got to jump off cliffs all the time and build your wings on the way down.
> —Ray Bradbury

What does this remind me of? *No matter what I do, it's not good enough.*

Joanne's Jealousy

Joanne's husband Bert is a busy man. He is not very demonstrative, and Joanne needs reminders, like traffic signs to assure her that he still loves her. Since Bert is so inscrutable, Joanne has begun listening in on his phone calls and going through the laundry for tell-tale signs before and after he leaves the house.

Thoughts about feelings: *My husband is so inconsiderate. He is always late and never lets me know when he will be home. I wonder if he is just working late or maybe he's having an affair. Maybe I am not attractive to him anymore. When he comes home and goes to sleep, I am going to go through his wallet and see if there are any receipts for gifts or restaurants that he has been visiting without me. I wonder if I should get a new haircut or buy a new dress. Maybe I can revive his interest in me.*

Feelings: *I am so scared my husband doesn't love me anymore. If he leaves, no one will ever love me again. I feel worthless and horrible. I can feel the tears welling up inside of me and the despair of not being lovable. My throat is so tight, I want to scream. My heart pounds every time I think of finding him with someone else. I can feel it throbbing in my ears. My whole body feels like it is going to explode.*

What does this remind me of? *No matter how much I do, it's never enough*

Patty and her Son

Patty has been a single mom for the last ten years. Her son Curt is

> We know the truth, not only by the reason, but also by the heart.
> —*Pascal*

a handful. Now 16, he rebels against all the household rules, won't carry his dishes from his room to the kitchen sink, and refuses to go to family counseling. Patty has resorted to constant nagging which has gotten her exactly nowhere. She is at her wits' end.

Thoughts about feelings: *My son is making me crazy. He never does what I tell him to do. He is so irresponsible; I just don't know what to do with him. If he just hadn't lost this last job, I would feel* *better. I am so worried about him. Maybe I need to lay down the law, get his father to speak to him, kick him out. But if I do that, he may never speak to me again, or go completely downhill.*

Feelings: *My son makes me so angry. When he is around, my body tenses up and I am on edge waiting for something horrible to happen. I have a knot in my stomach, just knowing that he will screw up somehow. I can feel the tears every time I think that I just have not been a very good parent.*

What does this remind me of? *It's all my fault*

If you find yourself stuck in your thoughts about your feelings, try to switch to focusing on your body and what it is experiencing. Do a "body scan." Start at the top of your head and let your mind wander down your body, noting what each part feels like. Write about your body's sensations even if that means repeating the same sentences over and over again to

> It is only with the heart that one can see rightly. What is essential is invisible to the eye.
> —*Antoine de Saint-Exupery*

distract your brain. "I am angry, my muscles are tense and my head is throbbing," *not* "George just insulted me," *not* "I would like to punch him in the mouth." "I am jealous of Sarah Lou," *not* "my husband is having an affair," *not* "I am going to confront him and get a divorce." Use soft music to further distance yourself from left brain activities.

Try to describe your feelings in some detail. If you are anxious, don't stop there. Ask what kind of anxiety it feels like, not why you are feeling it. Are you frightened of something? What? Do you feel like you are going to be crushed? Like you are going to fall down some deep dark hole? As if you are going to be chased, caught and injured? Don't worry about why. Why is not important.

Your body's sensations, not its thoughts, are the critical cues to focus on. They are trying to tell you something.

CHAPTER 13

◆ ◆ ◆ ◆ ◆

Step 3: Surface Your "Stuff"

Entering the Eye of the Storm

You can clutch the past so tightly to your chest, that it leaves your arms too full to embrace the present. *Jan Glidewell*

Focusing on sensations, for the healthy person with no old memories stored in the amygdala is a pleasant experience. These are the people who can kick back, relax, enjoy. But for those with a lot of "old stuff," the experience can be irritating.

If you are habitually anxious, you too may find it difficult to relax. You may be edgy when you focus on your feelings, irritable, off-key. You may be uncomfortable at any speed other than hyper fast. If so, the techniques in this chapter will guide you in how to dissolve these feelings little by little while you are feeling under pressure and uncomfortable, seized with panic attacks or obsessive thoughts.

Start a journal

The journal has a different purpose than the log. It can help you actually dissolve old emotional memories, in a slow, gentle manner.

In earlier chapters I talked about the recent discoveries from fMRI's that old emotional memories become "labile" (chemically

> The best way to get rid of a feeling that you don't want is to feel it.
> —*Elio Frattaroli*

unstable and easily altered or disrupted) each time they are triggered. There is evidence that resistance to feeling these sensations results in the memory undergoing another protein synthesis and being re-stored in the brain.

You can stop this process and allow the feelings to dissolve by journaling. Research shows that writing about or talking about one's *feelings* (as opposed to thoughts about feelings) produces significant improvement in emotional health.

- ♦ Students who were asked to feel and write about an extremely positive or negative experience, reported a decrease in obsessive thinking, improvement in working memory and improved GPA's compared to those who focused on the neutral topic of time management.

- ♦ College students who wrote about stressful events even improved their working memory skills when compared to those who simply recorded their daily events.

> Let your heart guide you. It whispers, so listen closely.
> —*The Land Before Time*

- ♦ Those who write about their emotions are less anxious and depressed and report greater life satisfaction than those who do not, according to a 12-year study of journal-writers.

Sieze the Moment

Start by writing about your feelings when you are feeling most distressed. Write about your feelings, not about your thoughts, write as fast as you can, and don't censor your words.

Use the built in discomfort from triggered feelings as a doorway through which you are able to retrieve old emotions and express them. If, for example, you are anxious whenever you open the bills or hear a particular voice on your message machine, anytime you experience any other event that is "evocative," don't rush by it. Stop and feel the sensation. Allow it to swell up and be discharged in small trembling sensations. Play the incident over in your images until they no longer evoke an emotional response.

Record your distressful sensations

Is there a particular incident that is attached to these emotions? What triggered them? Recall as many details as you can – images, feelings, sounds, smells or other sensations that you experienced during that incident, even if they were not directly related. Focus on the emotions that these thoughts, images and sounds evoke. Do you feel frightened? Angry? Hopeless? Write about these emotions as fully and completely as possible.

Ask yourself what these feelings remind you of. Do they feel familiar to you? Do you think you may have felt them many other times? Is this feeling a theme in your life? Write about that.

Focus on the actual physical sensations

Push yourself as far into your feelings as you can. If you begin to feel too upset and agitated, you can put your pen down and try to focus your attention to the actual physical sensations that you are

> Working in the fields is hard, but hunger is harder.
> —*Nilotic Proverb*

experiencing. Is your tummy in knots? Are your muscles tense?

Do you have a lump in your throat? Are you breathing faster? Is your heart pounding? Where are these feelings located? Feel them as fully as possible.

Back off from time to time

Don't push it beyond your limits. Back off when necessary and if the feelings become overwhelming. When you are calmer, go into the emotions, and feelings again, inching your way along. Focus as much as possible on the actual physical sensations you are experiencing, describing *what* you are feeling, not why. Try to describe the "texture" of the feeling. Exactly what is it? Are you angry because you feel controlled? Disrespected? Do you feel left out, as if others are encroaching on your space? Continue the process until you have no reaction, until you are completely calm when thinking about the previous incident.

This technique should give you some immediate relief, and within a few months, you should experience significant reduction in distress. It will also provide material that will help you identify your themes and get at the deeper pain that you may have stored, the pain that is bringing crises and painful relationships into your life.

> *When my mom ignored me one night, and it triggered old feelings of being ignored when I was little I went into that feeling and got really upset. I let out the feelings, cried a little and when I was done, I noticed a small change in the way I felt. Her ignoring me didn't bother me quite as much and I seemed overall a little happier.*

If you feel stuck

Look through the family picture album and notice what emotions are present with each picture or piece of memorabilia. Focus your attention on how your body is reacting, the various subtle sensations that come up as you study each picture. Are you calm and relaxed? Feeling spacey? Nervous? Tense? Zero in on where in your body the feelings are coming from. Are they in your torso? Extremities? Head? If you become extremely uncomfortable at any time, you can switch your focus to a pleasant scene until you calm down. Then resume the exercise.

Notice what makes you anxious in your day-to-day life. Is it opening the bills? Don't stop with the idea that you just don't have the money and that is why you are anxious. It is actually more likely that you are broke because you need to dissolve old feelings of insecurity. Ask yourself "what is the deeper feeling?" "What fear is buried inside?" "What does this remind me of?" "Have I ever felt this feeling before?" Remind yourself that not everyone is devastated by financial loss. Some people jumped off the Empire State Building in the midst of the Depression. Most did not. What is happening is that old fears are coming to the surface. When they are allowed to and are dissipated, your financial problems will dissolve with them.

Think about your political views and those of people you dislike. What is particularly upsetting to you? What political personalities are distressful? What are you feeling when you think about them? What do these feelings remind you of? What old feelings are they triggering?

When talking to close friends and family, after a run-in with the boss or co-worker, monitor your body's responses to what they are saying. What is upsetting? What is soothing? When it is upsetting, exactly what are you feeling? If it is fear, fear of what? If it is anger, what kind of anger? Remember, that whatever you feel, it is your feeling. Others can be in the exact same situation you are in and feel calm and relaxed.

Tell the truth when it is difficult to do so. Monitor your body's responses to the fear. What is it you are afraid of? What do you think you will lose if you tell the truth? Whenever we lie to hold onto something, we are struggling against the flow of what is supposed to be. If it is a relationship, let it go. Let the fear of being alone, of being unloved come to the surface.

Visit the website cinematherapy.com to select a movie that coincides with your mood. Rent the movie and while you are watching it, monitor your body's sensations. How are you feeling? What are the themes of the movie that evoke the strongest sensations? What do they remind you of?

Anger and Depression

If your main feeling of distress is anxiety you are lucky. Anger and depression are second order feelings and need to be treated a little differently.

All research indicates that going toward anger and depression can result in more anger and depression in a never-ending cycle. If you focus on "going into the feeling" you can "get stuck" there.

The trick is to use the feeling as a doorway to the sensation of anxiety, the source of the anger and depression, because anxiety is far more easily dissolved. Anger was a way you denied your powerlessness, of trying to get control; sadness and depression express that you gave up, that you were hopeless to improve your lot. Learned helplessness is a well-known phenomenon in psychological research. But

> Live the memory now. Give up any effort to control the experience. Consciously agree to feel whatever is happening. Go with the experience as far as possible.
> —Jean Jensen

underneath both feelings is the fear and anxiety of a child trying to get his or her needs met and failing. This is the feeling you want to reach

If you are angry, allow the feeling to ooze out and write about them for a few minutes. Ask yourself, what powerless feeling does this remind me of? Then, ask what fearful feeling does this remind me of? If something pops into your head, write about that.

If you are depressed, again, go toward the sadness and ask yourself what frightening feeling does this sadness remind me of? Focus on your physical sensations and write about them.

Do not linger in anger or sadness more than 15 minutes or so if you are not able to get to the feelings of anxiety. Go ahead and distract yourself. Pop a comedy in the VCR, go for a walk, talk to a friend, and try again another day.

Facing Phobias

Earlier I referred obliquely to one sensate-focused therapy that appears to be more effective than most others in the reduction of anxiety disorders, especially phobias. This approach is called systematic desensitization. While listed as and considered a behavioral therapy, it is, in all reality, a sensate-based process, and one you can do yourself.

The three basic steps involved in systematic desensitization include:

◆ Learning how to relax: Begin by selecting a tranquil image. Picture yourself tanning at the beach, floating in your swimming pool, lying in a hammock amidst a sea of green grass. Select any scene that produces a restful response.

◆ Creation of an anxiety hierarchy: Zero in on one feared situation that triggers your anxiety. Create a list of at least 10 anxiety-provoking scenes about that phobia ranging from the least to the most frightening.

◆ Imagination of the anxiety-provoking scenes: First put on some restful "new-age" type music. Sit in your favorite chair or lie down in a comfortable position. Get into a relaxed state by imagining your previously selected restful scene. Alternatively flex and relax each muscle group, starting with the top of your head, forehead, jaw, neck, shoulders, back chest, stomach, etc., until your entire body is at peace. Now, imagine the least anxiety-provoking scene in your hierarchy. Allow any mild feelings of distress to arise. Keep returning to the image of your restful scene. Repeat the process until the anxiety-provoking scene does not evoke any distressful feelings.

♦ Continue the process with each step of the anxiety hierarchy until you reach the most anxiety-provoking scene. Continue to allow the feeling to rise, and returning to restful scene whenever necessary.

After you are able to imagine each step of the hierarchy without anxiety, you may want to continue the technique in the actual feared situation. If you find yourself extremely fearful, especially if your anxiety does not allow you to relax, however, you may want to use the more cathartic technique described in the next chapter.

CHAPTER 14

◆ ◆ ◆ ◆ ◆

Step 4: Relinquish Control
And Surrender to Mother Nature

The best way out is always through.   *Robert Frost*

The cathartic experience is dramatic and is not the treatment of choice for the faint of heart. The experience is like going over Niagara Falls, the emotional equivalent of an orgasm. The distress builds steadily, levels off into a plateau stage and then explodes with emotion and sheer relief.

Catharsis can be done successfully on your own. After all, it as natural as throwing up because of food poisoning. In this case, you are instead expelling poison feelings.

> If you are a flag
> follow the wind.
> —*Swahili Proverb*

But if you are extremely frightened of your feelings and if you believe you can "let go" easier if you are with someone than you

163

can if you are alone, it should be done with a therapist or friend. Everyone differs on this issue, so you should go with your own sense of what is best for you. But if you choose to be with someone, it must be someone who is not disturbed by significant displays of emotion. If you choose this route, make sure that your supportive friend reads this section of the book and knows what to expect so they can truly be with you.

> Come to the edge he said; We are afraid they said. Come to the edge he said; They came. He pushed them; and they flew.
> —*Guillaume Appolinaire*

The drama of the cathartic experience is matched by the breadth and depth of the change it creates. So, if you are faced with extreme anxiety and fear, if you experience frequent panic attacks and sometimes feel as if you are going out of your mind, the cathartic experience can provide immediate and long-lasting relief.

Some people are able to get to catharsis on the first try; others take a bit longer and need a few practice runs. Still others will find that they prefer to take the slow boat to serenity. If you are able to use this technique to break through, however, you will probably be anxiety free for a considerable period of time. And, as the months and years go by, you will need to "do the process" less and less, and in time it will take only moments.

For the most immediate results, read the steps carefully and try them when you are in a great deal of emotional pain and substance free.

→**Recognize** when you start to experience emotional distress. Notice when you begin to be irritated with others, are edgy or nervous, emotional or sad. Note when you are attempting to control your environment or other people in it. Acknowledge your feelings without dismissing or negating them. This is your body giving you vital information for your emotional recovery—that some "old stuff" is being triggered and wants to come up and be discharged.

➜**Stop** yourself from using any and all addictions, and do not distract yourself. The point is not to dull or overwhelm the pain, but to make it as bad as possible—allow it to rise. Do not call friends, talk about how you are feeling, watch television, or do any of the other things you normally do to distract yourself.

➜**Isolate** yourself from all people and distractions. You must be in a safe place with no chance of being walked in on or interrupted. You must be in a place where you can "lose it"—cry scream, etc. and where you will not be seen or heard. Unplug the phone. Ask any housemates to go to the movie or take a ride in a car to a safe but unpopulated place. I recommend the far end of a busy shopping center to those who are uncomfortable in more remote locations.

➜**Turn** on soft or angry music if you wish—whatever will intensify the feeling you are experiencing and will drown out any noise distractions.

➜**Focus** on how your body feels, jitters in the stomach, ache in the heart, shaky nerves, discomfort in the pit of the stomach, constriction in your throat. Do not think about *why* you are feeling bad. Ask yourself the *"what am I feeling"* question. Try to turn off your brain by focusing on your body and its sensations.

➜**Write** about your body's feelings if you are having difficulty turning off your brain, and are stuck in obsessive thoughts. Do not switch into a meditative mode and attempt to clear your mind. Instead, deliberately focus on your body's sensations. Be as specific as possible about what you are feeling. What are you afraid of? What do you feel is going to happen? Don't

> It takes courage to be willing to stand still and feel what we must feel.
> —*Melody Beattie*

think about it; just ask yourself what the body sensations are telling you. Whenever you get off track, try to switch back to the focus on your body. Write about it even if it means writing the same thing over and over

➔**Go** toward the pain: make it as bad as possible; stay with it as long as possible. Try to go the center of the pain.

➔**Feel** the tears wanting to come up. Focus on them, and allow them to come. As the tears come, stay focused on your body and its feelings. Allow yourself to have disastrous thoughts. This is normal. It is old feelings coming to the surface, feelings that you had at a time when you were a dependent child.

➔**Understand** the fear. You may at this point begin to experience overwhelming fear. This feeling is exactly what you experienced—and stored—as a child and is not related to any danger you are in at the present time. Be clear about this. Nothing bad is going to happen to you if you allow your feelings to come up and overwhelm your brain. Only good will come of it. Going to the center of the pain will not kill you. This is the "old stuff" that needs to be discharged. It feels so terrible because when you were a tiny child, had no one taken care of you, you might have died. It is the child's feelings that are still inside.

➔**Ask** yourself "what does this remind me of." [5] Often one or two words or a phrase will usually come to the surface. What the words are is not important at this stage. Asking the question is simply a matter of connecting the present day circumstances that triggered the pain with the old stored pain.

➔ **Go back** as far as you can in time with the feelings. Ask "what very old childhood feeling – *not what experience* – does this remind me of?"

➔**Drop** to the center of the pain (the depths of despair). It should feel as if you were in free fall, like dropping hundreds of feet in a

---

[5] *This is an essential part of the process. Making the emotional connection to the past by "feeling" the theme is generally the key to a successful cathartic experience.*

roller coaster or elevator. It has also been described as an emotional orgasm. While the moments leading up to the explosion are excruciatingly painful, the second you go over the edge you will feel at the same time, great relief. As the emotion comes pouring out, you will feel calmer and calmer, as if the electricity is draining out of your body.

> When you come to the edge of all the light you know, and are about to step off into the darkness of the unknown, faith is knowing one of two things will happen: There will be something solid to stand on, or you will be taught how to fly.
> —Barbara J. Winter

This is the final stage in letting go of the intellect and allowing the feelings to surface. To observers who haven't experienced this deep process, it may appear that the person is going out of control.

Listen to three eloquent descriptions of the experience:

The first is from *Facing the Wolf*, a book by Theresa Sheppard Alexander:

> *It was as if I had returned to the moment of trauma and felt the actual terror of that long ago moment.*
>
> *I went into an internal downward spiral. . . . It was as if a door had opened into the past. . . . My whole body and feelings were catapulted back. . . . The dam burst*

The second from Richard Berendzen's riveting book *Come Here*.

> *Tears ran down his stubby cheeks. His bass voice cracked. And from his barrel chest came a groan that froze my skin—it was the muffled scream of a small boy echoing through time.*
>
> *My heart raced. I held my chest. Never before had I felt such throbbing, thundering pain. My face flushed, The*

room spun. As images sped around me and through me I choked on silent screams. This was cataclysmic. Like entering a warp in space and time. I catapulted back more than four decades. Trapped between the shadow of a boy and the shell of a man, I relived every sordid afternoon all at once.

And from Jon Du Pre's wonderful book, *The Prodigal Father:*

How much time off do you need?" I shot back even louder this time. How much space?" Louder. 'How long can a person be sick?" Louder. "What made you sick, old man? Were you just sick of being a father? Sick of being needed?" Louder. "You make me sick!" Louder "You people who think you can quit on the people who love them just because you think you're sick. Being a chicken shit is not a disease, Dad. I'll tell you who's sick. I'm sick! I'm sick of your excuses! Quitters like you make me want to puke!" Louder, until my voice cracked and I was hissing . . . "Quitter!" I heard myself shriek, but it sounded like someone else, off in the distance, beyond the ringing in my ears. I heard, "You're no lawyer!" Then, "You're clients didn't love you!" Then, "We loved you! Marq and Daryl loved you!" Then " . . . fucking quitter!" The last one came out like vomit, like the dry heaves when you think your eyes are going to pop out of their sockets.

Then his head dropped. The muscles in his shoulders constricted and his neck stiffened. The old man on the concrete bench let out a wail like I'd never heard a human make. And he sobbed so hard it cause him to quake on his seat. This lasted 20, 30, 40 minutes . . . longer than that. Then it subsided to a whimper.

When you experience the cathartic process, you are not going out of your mind. You are simply allowing the healing process to arise within the body. Only the intellect has lost control—it has given up its power to the innate wisdom of the body.

➔**Stay** down at the bottom of the pain as long as you can—for an hour or more if possible. Continue to focus on how your body feels every time you begin to "lighten up." Focus on the general feeling of despair, hopelessness, fear, not the reasons why. If a phrase surfaced when you asked "what does this remind me of," repeat this phrase a few times to trigger you back to the depths of the pain. Each time you begin to emerge, repeat the phrase. Do this until the phrase evokes no more feelings, until it is completely neutral. This is the experience of dissolving old feelings.

Dealing with Fear

The average person who registers for a *Therapist Within™ Seminar* spends 25-50% of his or her waking hours – four to eight hours per day per person – either in emotional turmoil, or trying to prevent uncomfortable feelings from surfacing. Most people are terrified of their powerful feelings. Anything seems better than experiencing them. Why do we use all our formidable skills to keep the old, poisonous feelings inside?

Old childhood stuff often feels as if we are going to die. Events that would be trivial to an adult can be terrifying to a child that is

> Some people are so afraid to die that they never begin to live.
> —Henry Van Dyke

dependent on others for its physical, emotional, and spiritual survival. Being left in a hospital, getting lost, witnessing violence at home, anything that shakes a child's sense of safety and security can be reasonably interpreted as "I am going to die." The facts of the experience are irrelevant. Imagine being asleep in your bed when three masked robbers armed to the teeth stage a home invasion, stick an Uzi in your face and demand all your money. The fear would be overwhelming, roughly equivalent to a child hearing a drunk parent stagger up the stairs, not knowing if he or she will pass by your room without incident or stumble in and molest you.

Soul damage can be just as traumatic. Criticism – both spoken and unspoken – of *who* a child is, is aimed like a spear at his soul. The feelings that accumulate when a mother clings to her son as a substitute for a good relationship with her husband; when a father browbeats his artistic son to become a tough football hero; when parents expect a child to live up to the standards set by an earlier sibling, damage the soul.

> *It was very difficult to deal with because I never knew what kind of emotions she was going to throw at me from one minute to the next. I didn't feel at all comfortable around her. I felt like I somehow needed to take charge, but I couldn't because she wouldn't allow it, I was to be seen and not heard. She had a very fast and quick backhand.*

> *My father was not home. He was a businessman who commuted to San Francisco. So my mother was very much a controller. And it was always out to dinner at a good restaurant and there were drinks, and it would make me a nervous wreck because I knew she was driving under the influence, and not knowing how she was going to react to anyone.*

> I will face my fear. I will permit it to pass over me and through me. And when it has gone past, I will turn the inner eye to see its path. Where the fear has gone, there will be nothing. Only I will remain.
> —*Frank Herbert Dune*

> *She could be very mean. My mother became a very mean person during that time. She would basically be very verbally demeaning, very mean, very physical. I was very frightened. Very frightened. But then when we would finally get to the point where she had enough to drink and enough Valium, then she would lay down then I knew I felt at peace because then*

I felt I could be free and I didn't have to worry about getting hit or slapped.

Many of us equate letting our feelings out with having a nervous breakdown. Having our thinking brain in charge and in control is what we are used to. It is what we believe constitutes sanity. To allow our feelings to come to the surface feels as frightening as if we were about to be swept over Niagara Falls.

> No one ever told me that grief felt so like fear.
> —C. S. Lewis

"I am afraid if I allow myself to feel the full extent of my anxiety, I will go crazy and not be able to 'come back,'" said Sally in a *Therapist Within™ Seminar.* It is a common, but unfounded fear.

I had a fear of finding out what was deep in there. Because I was afraid to find out if it was really truly going to hurt, and I didn't want to have any more hurt, because I felt I'd been living with hurt for so many years, from childhood through my adult life, I'd had so much hurt until I had taken your class. And realizing that I had lived this for 40 + years. And I didn't want to confront that. I was afraid to confront it. And that scared the hell out of me.

I was afraid that once I went through the process, and I was down deep that I wouldn't come out of it. I felt that I wouldn't be able to stop, or that it would throw me into some type of avenue that would make me so afraid I just felt I would be trapped. The reality after the process was how much lighter I felt.

We are not "losing control" when we detach from the thinking brain and plug into the emotional brain. We are simply allowing nature to do

> Growing up is not a gentle process – no wonder so many people are not really interested and would rather have a "fast fix".
> —Dr. Eric Marcus

what it was designed to do and what our body wants to do – expel the original feeling by expressing it in its entirety so that *it will go away and never come back.* Detaching from the thinking brain is the very definition "Letting Go."

We are afraid the explosion will be volcanic. The turmoil you are experiencing has, in all likelihood, built up considerable internal pressure over the years. How much depends on whether or not you have ever released any of the original feelings, how effective your efforts have been at keeping it underground, and how long they have been locked inside.

The paradox, of course, is that those who have been highly successful in ignoring the distress and pushing it away, will, in the end, be in more turmoil. In our flight from pain, we actually create more of it. The initial explosion, when it comes, can be frightening, especially if you don't understand what is happening.

Listen to one brilliant and famed scientist who chose his academic major only because it was the hardest, and earned his PhD in physics and astronomy from Harvard. Long ago, even before his mother had molested him, beckoning him with those fateful words "come here," Richard had learned to live in his mind. Now, almost 50 years later, as he entered the room where the abuse had begun, the feelings he had bottled up for so long came crashing down.

> The way I see it, you can either run from it, or learn from it.
> —Rafikki to Simba in Disney's The Lion King

> *"When I walked into the middle bedroom, the first thing I saw was the unmade bed. Like an echo of death, the sheets still held the indentation of my father's body. Seeing that shape was the shout that brought down the avalanche. . . .*

> *Like a thundering mountainside of snow, I was smothered by feelings I thought had ended forty years before. Panic, fear, confusion, helplessness, anguish and desperation jackknifed inside me.*

This time I could not escape. Every emotion I had ever buried, every thought I had ever suppressed came back with unimaginable force and intensity. . . As images sped around and through me, I choked on silent screams. I wasn't remembering, I was reliving the abuse by my mother.

Yes, the distress of expressing the feelings you have held in so long can be extreme. They will feel exactly the way they did when you were a child. You lived through these feelings as a tiny helpless baby and you will live through them again. Human beings do not die as a result of expressing their pain. If you don't believe this, check out the obituaries. In fact, far more of us die years too early because we *don't* let our feelings out!

> The only pain that can be avoided is the pain that comes from trying to avoid the pain. Problems are not caused by distressing events, but by our perceived need to avoid the emotional impact of what happens to us.
> —R. D. Laing

The cost of serenity is the willingness to walk into the pain instead of running from it. The willingness to re-live the original pain precisely as you felt it before it was stored . . . to go back to being a young child for a few minutes, and express the emotions exactly as you would have then, had you been allowed to . . . to chose the sharp momentary pain of the surgeon's knife rather than living a slow, agonizing death from an emotional cancer.

It means making room and time for the pain to emerge, understanding that it is temporary and that it is leaving you, never to return.

But the payoff for your courage is immense. It is

♦ the joy of walking in the world without fear, of waking up every morning knowing that the universe is going to bring you everything you need to be healthy, joyful, and whole. Of no longer being afraid of other people nor of their behavior, having no triggers, no longer needing to control in order not to get hurt. It means trusting yourself to attract and be attracted to exactly those people and events that will make you healthy in the long run.

♦ A life lived in harmony with the world, without struggle, knowing that the way to serenity is surrender. Knowing that if you stop fighting your circumstances and feel the direction of the universe, you can float rather than claw your way through life.

♦ Self-assurance, self-determination and self-direction, being clear about who you are and where you are going, being free of self-doubt, being comfortable in your own skin. It means not having to ask others what you should do because you know what is best for you. It means knowing when your body wants food, and when it needs rest, when to go to the doctor, and when not. It means to trust in your instincts, to know when your instincts are warning you of some new danger and when old pain is trying to come out. It means automatically setting boundaries and sticking to them without guilt.

> The harder you fall, the higher you bounce.
> —Unknown

♦ Freedom from anxiety, angst, phobia's, anger, depression, dysfunctional relationships and multiple life crises, without having to work at it, without having to keep feelings in check or dull them with drugs and other addictions

> Heaven knows we need never be ashamed of our tears, for they are rain upon the blinding dust of Earth, overlaying our hard hearts.
> —Charles Dickens

♦ Knowledge that pain is not pointless, that as soon as you go through it, it will disappear. It is knowing that if anxiety begins to arise, or a crisis appears around the corner, that it is just Mother Nature's way of triggering some more "old stuff" in order to get rid of it and make you whole.

♦ Freedom from having to work on your issues, from obsessive thinking and "analysis paralysis." It means to sleep peacefully, and an end to insomnia. Freedom from needing to think about your issues, engage in endless discussions, read self-help books, or pursue endless therapy, so you can get on with your life!

To get there, requires only that you be willing to seize the moment when Mother Nature presents it and have a modicum of courage when you do so.

CHAPTER 15

♦ ♦ ♦ ♦ ♦

Step 5: Restore the Mind/Body Connection
Getting in Touch With Your Body

My patients enter therapy completely disconnected from their bodies and unaware of the integral connection between certain physical sensations and their own emotional state.
Theresa Sheppard Alexander

As you begin to step into your feelings, you may have an overwhelming sense that you are in a foreign country. All the old problems you have ignored – lack of sleep, chronic illness, an impaired immune system, lack of energy will come to the surface.

Don't be discouraged. One of the most significant side benefits to getting rid of your "old stuff" is significant improvement in your physical health. Why? First, the body's response to the stress that accompanies triggering your emotional baggage is both destructive and cumulative. Becoming tranquil begins to reverse the process. Second, when you are able to feel and understand your most subtle sensations at their inception and take corrective action before they grow to critical proportions you can head off much of the disease process.

Stress and the Disease Process

While modern medicine has successfully attacked infectious causes of disease, the rate of illnesses with strong emotional components continues to soar. For the first time in history, the major causes of death and disease – high blood pressure, heart disease, arthritis, cancer – are stress-related. The Practice Directorate estimates that 75-90% of all visits to primary care physicians are psychogenic in origin. What is the relationship between these disorders and our emotions?

> Stress is so unremitting for many people that they don't even recognize it any more, and this lack of sensitivity can be cumulatively dangerous.
> —Kenneth Pelletier

The General Adaptation Syndrome

The ability to respond quickly and effectively to occasional emergencies is truly wondrous. But nature clearly has intended stress should be short term. We are designed to pay attention to discomfort, learn the lesson and do something different. If we don't, in time, the body's natural coping system begins to collapse.

Canadian endocrinologist Hans Selye described our response to stress as the General Adaptation Syndrome and detailed the characteristics of its three stages – alarm, resistance and exhaustion

> *Alarm* – includes the body's original response to threat as it floods the body with the hormones adrenalin and noradrenalin, allowing us to fight back or flee.
>
> *Resistance* – involves the body attempts to cope with the assault by adjusting or resisting the threatening experience.

Although the intense arousal of the alarm stage ebbs, the physical arousal remains above normal and the body's ability to resist new stressors is impaired.

Exhaustion – when the stress becomes chronic, prolonged and unabated as it does when old emotional memories are constantly triggered, it activates a second endocrine pathway and releases hormones called corticosteriods. Though helpful in the short-run, in time these hormones weaken important body systems, damage the kidneys, lower immunity and increase susceptibility to physical illness.

Specific Damage from Prolonged Stress

Though the research on the relationship between stress and illness is still in its infancy, results so far have documented a connection between emotional disorders and the following diseases.

Hypertension and Heart Disease.
Cortoids that circulate in the blood stream make tiny tears in the arterial walls. As the body attempts to repair them with cholesterol plaques, a type of scar tissue, the arteries harden.

Many individuals behave as though they are anesthetized from the neck down and seldom take the time to listen to the wisdom of the body.
—*Kenneth Pelletier*

Brain Aging and Memory Loss. Over-activation of these same hormones accelerates aging and degeneration of brain structures including the hippocampus – our primary factual memory system.

The Immune System, Colds and Cancer. The immune system, the body's surveillance system, is also severely damaged when exposed to the long-term stress that accompanies repression. The number of white blood cells decreases making us more vulnerable to colds and even cancer.

Auto-immune diseases. Auto-immune diseases including diabetes, arthritis, lupus, and fibromyalgia appear to occur when a damaged immune system, loses the ability to tell friend from foe and begins to attack the body itself.

Sleep Disorders. The effects of stress and repression of feelings is exacerbated by our huge sleep debt. Americans get 90 minutes too little sleep a night. This adds up not only to more accidents on the highway and workplace, but in too few REM dreams, which are required to process the emotional content of the day. There is convincing evidence that sleep disorders such as insomnia can increase the risk of high blood pressure, coronary artery disease, heart failure and stroke, obesity and diabetes.

It's Too Late, Baby

By the time we are visibly sick, in one sense, it is too late. It is the tragedy behind our inability to discern and respect our physical sensations. While clinicians concern themselves only when there are clinical signs of disease (stage 4) internal signs of distress appear much earlier. In other words, though your doctor can't "see" the disease process until Stage 4, if you are aware of your feelings, you can *sense* it!

> We should put out fire while it is still small.
> —Kenya Proverb

Where are you on the health scale? Do you have symptoms of disease? Or are you energetic, joyful, excited, serene, and an active participant in life? Do you rarely get sick, or do you catch every cold to which you are exposed? Do you believe that being tired and depressed is just part of growing older? Or do you understand that it sometimes takes the accumulation of years of abuse for the symptoms of illness to appear?

The critical message from recent research is: ***you are not powerless in the face of the disease process.*** You have in your hands, in being able to detect and respond to your most subtle physical sensations, the power to derail much potential disease before it even begins.

If you are not as healthy as you would like to be, start paying more attention to your physical sensations and the systems Mother Nature has put in place to notify you of how the system – your body – is supposed to run if it is to be in peak condition.

Biological rhythms and sleep

During the day and even throughout the night, there is a natural and subtle ebb and flow of mental and physical energy. These cycles, which are regulated primarily by sunlight, occur in approximately 90-minute cycles of activity and rest. In addition, more than 100 physical processes peak and dip within any 24 hours including sensitivity to visual, auditory, taste and smell stimuli, pain sensitivity, and physical strength.

What happens when we ignore our biological clock and pay attention instead to the invented one?

♦ It is one more brick in the wall between operating according to internal signals and operating according to external ones.

♦ It increases the likelihood of accidents. Both the 3-Mile Island and Chernoble disasters occurred during the swing shifts.

♦ Disruptions in sleep can cause disruptions in mood, reaction time and complex motor skills as well as harmful changes in metabolic and endocrine functioning, and abnormal glucose levels.

> The willingness to accept responsibility for one's own life is the source from which self-respect springs.
> —Joan Didion

Take some time to get familiar with your biological clock and cater to it as much as possible. Are you a morning person or a night person? When are you the most energetic mentally? Physically? How much sleep do you need? Most of us need eight to nine hours of sleep a night (more if you are a teenager).

Note how often you feel mental fatigue. It can be a sign that the brain simply needs time to process and store information before it is ready to effectively absorb anything new. Continuing to stuff your brain is self-defeating, like writing on a blackboard when it is already crammed with information. The brain – primarily the hippocampus, your factual memory system – simply pushes out the old information to make room for the new. It is a zero-sum game.

By signaling you that it is fatigued, your brain is giving you an important message. Enough already! Take a walk, do something physical, take a 30-60 or even a 90 minute break. If that makes you feel guilty and lazy, remind yourself that your brain, like your muscles, continues to operate after a workout, finishes processing the old stuff and prepares for a new round of intellectual calesthenics.

> *When I first learned about biological rhythms, I didn't really believe it, but after experimenting, I am convinced. A few weeks ago I was at the coffee house to study for my political science exam. I stayed there for the entire evening and for the first 90 minutes I studied intensely. Then I got up, stretched, ordered something, chatted with a couple of people for another 90 minutes before I went back to studying. I was more alert, which surprised me. After I got home, I decided to sleep to lock the information in. Then, the next day, decided to follow your instructions and not study right before the exam. Well, I took the exam and did awesome! My essay was the second highest in the class even though essays aren't really my thing. I will definitely study this way in the future instead of cramming and pulling all-nighters.*

Note your physical symptoms when you are tired. Do you feel as if you are coming down with a cold or other illness? Get extra sleep and drink plenty of liquids. Do you eat when you are actually tired? If you are physically fatigued, need a nap and can take one, do it. If it is night time, sleep. Your body knows what it needs.

Do you feel mentally alert but still, your arms and legs feel like limp noodles? If your muscles are weak, if you have trouble falling asleep, you may need additional minerals. Be sure you get them and keep track of the results.

Are you always exhausted? If you eat many refined carbohydrates, drink alcohol, or have had antibiotics lately, try strengthening your immune system with acidophilus, the natural, good bacteria that keep the bad ones at bay and other natural remedies. You can get acidophilus at most health-food stores. Buy the kind that needs refrigeration.

If these changes don't help, it may be time to see a doctor. Remember, the healthier you are, the more energy you will have to stick to your commitment to change.

Coffee and Alcohol

> Just one cup of coffee a day in the morning affects brain wave patterns during sleep at night.
> —*Joseph Glenmullen*

If you are chronically tired, but drink 10 cups of coffee a day, you may be oblivious to the symptoms of a potentially deadly disease until it's too late. If you need alcohol to put you to sleep, you will never get to the root cause of those racing thoughts that keep you up half the night.

Coffee and alcohol mask important messages from Mother Nature, and both leach calcium and other important minerals from the system (calcium helps you sleep). If you stop consuming caffeine and are exhausted, it is *not* a message that you need caffeine! It is a message that your body is not operating in peak condition and may be suffering from a chronic illness.

If you don't think you can handle giving up caffeine cold-turkey, don't. Instead, begin to decrease your intake of caffeine slowly. Fill your cup with ¾ caffeinated coffee, ¼ de-cafe for the first week. The second week, try ½ and ½. The third week, reduce your intake by another ¼. At the same time, increase your intake of vitamins, and, if you feel tired and drained, pursue techniques that will boost your immune system, like pro-biotics (acidophilus, multi-dophilus that you can get at most health-food stores), or see a doctor who is trained in not only Western medicine, but nutrition as well.

Note how you feel after consuming alcohol. Alcohol is a central nervous system and immune system depressant. Even small amounts of alcohol (and other products like sugar and white flour) depress the immune response for from four to thirty-six hours! Again, probiotics and other immune system boosters can be helpful in countering the effects if you cannot give them up entirely.

Monitor how your body feels after taking corrective action. Are you an alcoholic or a carbo-holic? Next time you drink alcohol and want another, eat a sweet instead. Did this satisfy you for at least half an hour? An hour? If so, if you didn't care which you had, you could be addicted to carbohydrates instead of alcohol. The solution is to begin eating more protein, etc. See how that works.

Food

If you ignore your body's hunger signals, you will never be able to select the right foods for your body chemistry. Before you eat, ask yourself if you are really hungry. Note the feelings in your body that are signaling you to eat. Are they physical or emotional? Do you really want to eat, or do you need to talk to a friend, get yourself out of a boring routine, or have a good weep-fest?

Before you eat, spend at least 15 minutes focusing on what your body is trying to tell you. Are you having hunger pangs or is the hunger emotional? What might satisfy your emotional hunger? Do you need to cry? To kick a concrete wall? Don't think about it; just picture yourself having selected different options. Which feel relaxing to you? Which bring on that "ahhhhhh" feeling? What will give you real relief, not the temporary relief of an addiction?

How do you feel immediately after eating? If you are sometimes too full, slow down. Take your time. It takes 20-30 minutes for your brain to process the information that you have had enough to eat. Are you hungry shortly after eating? It may be a reaction to a particular kind of food. How do you feel if you eat primarily meat and leafy green vegetables? Do you feel different if you eat carbohydrates such as pasta, rice, potatoes, corn, or bread – the white stuff? Try meals that are primarily made up primarily of carbohydrates one day, of mostly protein. another. Note how you feel, and how quickly you are hungry again. Perhaps you are eating too many carbohydrates, or not enough protein. Experiment with different foods and note your reactions, how satiated you are, how soon you want to eat again.

Insulin Resistance

If, once you start to eat you have a hard time stopping, or if you tend to gain weight around the middle of the body, you may be insulin resistant, or what doctors are now calling Syndrome X. Insulin resistance is a pre-diabetic condition in which the body dumps excessive quantities of insulin into the system even at the mere sight of food. Since excess insulin is a precursor not only to diabetes but also heart disease, and other debilitating illnesses, addressing the issue is critical to your well-being.

If you or others in your biological family are insulin resistant, you can take corrective action and dramatically increase your insulin sensitivity. Eat more protein and green, leafy vegetables, decrease or eliminate simple carbohydrates, such as sugar, flour, pasta and bread – the white stuff. Limit your intake of starchy carbohydrates such as beans, rice, peas and corn. Drink more water, increase your intake of fiber, walk for at least 30 minutes a day or otherwise increase your exercise regime, take chromium picolonate (any health food store can help you), and/or go on a hypocaloric diet (500 or fewer calories) for three days. Monitor how your body feels after each of these changes. The American Dietetic Association is *not* the expert when it comes to your diet. Your body is.

Exercise

If you don't have a favorite exercise, experiment now. There is one that will fit you. It may be walking, bicycling, sports, dancing, swimming, or classes at the gym. It may be yoga, tai chi or a self-defense class. There is evidence that lack of oxygen may be involved in producing some of the pain of autoimmune diseases such as fibromyalgia. By increasing the oxygen available to the system, exercise might help.

If you are depressed, take a walk in the early morning sunshine. This simple act, along with a healthy diet can increase the serotonin in the blood system quickly and naturally without any of the side effects of psychotropic drugs.

Note how and when you exercise and how you feel after each session, note any aches and pains, any feeling of exhilaration. Take it easy if your energy level is low. As your health improves, you will have more energy. Monitor your body's responses each week and don't expect immediate results. It can take as much as two to three months for the antidepressant effects of exercise to kick in.

The Power of Expression

And don't forget. Expressing your feelings instead of bottling them up not only improves your emotional health, it has a significant secondary effect on your physical health as well.

186

♦ When people were given the opportunity to express their feelings either by writing or speaking about them, there was a decrease in Epstein-Barr antibodies.

♦ People who write about their feelings after experiencing a stressful event increase one of the important cells of the immune system that combats infection.

♦ When college students wrote essays about their difficulties adjusting to college, their immune function improved in the following months, compared to a control group that wrote about superficial subjects.

> Gentlemen, I want you to know that you're looking at the darndest healing machine that's ever been wheeled into this hospital
> —Norman Cousins,

Implementing these deep changes in our habits will take time. But health requires that we resist the urge to treat symptoms instead of uprooting the cause of disease. By escalating the struggle between what nature wants – to get our attention – and what we want – an immediate cessation of the pain we may win the battle but we will lose the war. It's time we declared a truce with Mother Nature.

From Turmoil to Tranquility

CHAPTER 16

◆ ◆ ◆ ◆ ◆

Step 6: Rehearse
And Get Your Life Back

Trust thyself. Every heart vibrates to that iron string.
Ralph Waldo Emerson

Though the aftermath of all of these sensate processes is similar, the timing very different. The results of the cathartic process are more immediately felt and far more dramatic, and so I will focus on the results of this technique. You can expect the same results for the gentler processes as well, but they will emerge over a longer period of time.

Often the results of the cathartic experience are immediate and quite exquisite. You may be filled with relief, peace and joy. If this is your experience, savor it. This is what it feels like to be healthy. Bathe in the sensation. Make it yours and lock it into your memory so that you can find your way home the next time anxiety hits.

Other times you may have a sensation that you have just been through the wringer. Some of those who have been through it report feeling drained, exhausted, even as if they have a hangover. Some report having no energy, wanting to rest, float in the pool, do no housework, take a light walk, etc. Catharsis is a significant emotional experience. You have demonstrated great courage in allowing these feelings to surface and dissolve. Pamper yourself for a few days. Get a massage, walk slowly, soak up the sun, or putter around. Just let your body talk to you and tell you what it needs. Let it heal.

How Long Will It Last?

This first period of serenity after catharsis may last a few days, or a few months, depending on the length and depth you were able to achieve and the degree of emotional baggage you have. But don't be discouraged if and when discomfort returns. It only means that you have more "infection" to get rid of, more emotional memories to dissolve, and that as soon as you do, the tranquility will return. Remember that it took years to accumulate these stored memories, it will take some time to get rid of them. As you continue, the process will take less and less time, the sessions less frequent, and the times in between more serene. Eventually, you will go for years without a single pang of anxiety, with every day filled with joy.

> And what do we teach our children in school? We teach them that two and two make four and that Paris is the capital of France. When will we also teach them what they are? You should say to each of them: Do you know what you are? You are unique. In all the world there is no other child exactly like you. In the millions of years that have passed there has never been a child like you . . . Yes, you are a marvel.
> —Pablo Casals

It Wasn't My Fault

Many people in the midst of the bottom of the pain realize—they just suddenly *know*—emotionally in their gut, not just intellectually—that they weren't responsible for the pain they had experienced as a child. It wasn't their fault. It is clear as they feel the severity of the pain, that it wasn't right to allow a little helpless innocent child to go through that kind of experience. It is almost as if a switch is thrown. Whenever another person exhibits that same behavior, you notice. It rings a bell. No longer does one "put up with" that kind of behavior. Rather than being an attractor, it becomes a repellent.

Repeat the experience as often as you can, whenever the opportunity arises. Keep writing in your journal. You will soon notice that the periods of discomfort are shorter and less frequent, the periods of joy longer and more pronounced. Experiences that once caused great anxiety will pass without your even noticing them. Circumstances that would trigger your need to control may have vanished. Later you may realize that you are no longer upset by the behavior of a significant other or boss, no longer "shook" by unexpected occurrences.

Be aware that you may be particularly prone to painful episodes when involved in new relationships. This is normal. We are never so vulnerable as we are in a new relationship that mimics our childhood experiences. Don't try to force anything. You don't need to manufacture opportunities to practice the technique, just allow circumstances in your life to dictate when it is time to get rid of the next set of emotional baggage. The discomfort will arise naturally when you are ready for the next experience.

It took Roger a couple of months and the loss of a job to beak through. Even though he had practiced the cathartic process, when the anxiety got bad, when he had a fight with his boss or his wife, he still couldn't quite make it over the edge. He was stuck in his head.

> *The day I got fired, my wife threatened to leave. She was sick and tired of the chaos of our lives and my surly attitude. What I really wanted to do was hit her, drive the*

car 150 miles an hour, take a machine gun to the boss, get drunk or commit suicide. Or maybe all of these things.

But because I knew that neither my boss nor my wife was responsible for my pain, I knew it had to be old stuff, I finally just let it all go. I didn't really have any choice.

It was the most horrible pain I had ever experienced. I was sure I was cracking up. And, in retrospect, I sort of was. I was letting go of all the abuse I had suffered as a child. All the beatings, all the humiliation, all the fear. It all came pouring out.

Afterward I wondered what had taken me so long. What was I so afraid of? Life afterwards was so much calmer, so much happier. I wish I had known what to do sooner. It might have saved me lots of jobs that I lost, and my first marriage."

Follow Your Feelings

As you recover from emotional distress, you will begin to appreciate and protect the feelings, the subtle physical sensations that are your lifeline to happiness and health. You may take up yoga or get regular massages. You will be able to take advantage of the short-cuts that emotionally healthy people make every day – checking in with your body's messages instead of thinking things to death.

Use your physical sensations to help you make decisions. Imagine each alternative – see yourself having selected choice one. Picture yourself acting out the decision.

Keep your ear tuned to discomfort of any type. If you are tempted to behave in an angry or revengeful way, it is old stuff coming to the surface. If you are tempted to lie, cheat, steal, or do anything that you consider immoral, it is old stuff coming to the surface. Go into the feeling and let it come and dissolve.

Listening to Your Mind AND Body

As you encounter different experiences with your spouse, significant other, or children, listen not only with your verbal brain but with your emotional brain as well. Remember the people who had damaged the part of the brain that understood words, but were better able to read faces? If you are caught in an argument with a loved one, stop listening to the words, and feel what they are saying to you – what is the feeling behind the words? Remember, at the base of anger is fear. What do you feel they are afraid of? On the other hand, if they are triggering anger or fear in you, what exactly is that feeling? What old feeling does their emotion remind you of?

When your children tell you they aren't doing drugs, what does your gut say? If a new boyfriend tells you to relax when you try to resist their advances, what does your intuition tell you? If your spouse tells you she is not running around, what does your body signal? That she is? Is that your old stuff talking to you? Go into the pain, dissolve it and then check again. Keep on dissolving the old pain until you are calm with whatever the truth is. It is then that you will know what to do. You will know the truth.

General Body Sensations

Practice getting more in touch with your body's most subtle sensations. When you take a shower, feel the water spraying on your skin. If you have a pulsating shower-head, experiment with different modes. Just feel the different sensations. When you walk in the sun, feel the heat on your skin. Notice the difference between the parts of the body that are covered and those that are not. Notice how the breeze affects different body parts, you legs, arms, face. Experiment, spend some time every day focusing on how your body feels.

Savor your meals. Note the flavor, texture, color, aroma of each bite. Chew slowly, and when you plan a meal, make sure it consists of a variety of sensual experiences.

Spend time appreciating the color of the sky, the rustling of the leaves, the song of a bird, the feel of grass under your feet. Once, in my days as a workaholic, as I was getting ready to leave for a training session with teachers, I suddenly burst into tears. The morning TV program was just signing off with a montage of flowers, grasses and butterflies, soft music and rich colors. Mother Nature was talking to me. Slow down, she said. Something important is missing in your life. I was not then of a mind to listen.

Sensuality

If you are involved in a sexual relationship, practice sensuality. Get your creative imagination going, rent a sensual movie such as *A Man and a Woman* or get some books that are sensate-focused. These should deliberately not be erotica-focused. I have no argument with erotica, but the use of such materials is often used to override physical sensations with an adrenaline rush. For the time being, we are trying to increase sensitivity, not decrease it.

> The soul leads us to embrace our fate.
> —Sir Thomas Moore

Instead, focus on your entire body and its responses, not just the sexual ones. Use a feather to lightly brush your partner's body. Listen to your own body when you are being gently stimulated. Slow down; take the opportunity to savor the subtlest sensations.

As you continue to connect with your body, you will find it easier and easier to connect with your emotions.

The Power of the System

When you go through the process, and feel relief, perhaps for the first time in your life, you will begin embrace and appreciate the wisdom and dominance of Mother Nature, and stop trying to control her. Think of the chaos that would ensue if the universe ran according to any one human being's desires? Which person and whose desires would prevail? How would conflicting wants and needs be sorted out? Given that no one person can ever know all the pieces of the universe or how they interact, isn't it better if we didn't try quite so hard to control nature, if we allowed nature to more often prevail? It is entirely possible, in fact it is likely that

- The Universe is exactly as nature has designed it to be for the maximum survival and development of all.

- That Mother Nature is wiser than we, especially when it comes to the critical issue of the health and survival of the entire system.

- That nature is geared first toward long-term and global issues rather than those that are short term and individual

- That nature is stronger and will win in the long run anyway, so we might as well look for ways to work with her.

- That most of our distress comes from trying to fight a losing battle:

Coming back to your body is like coming back home. It is in the fullest sense, coming back to yourself, to being the whole, healthy person you were meant to be.

From Turmoil to Tranquility

CHAPTER 17

♦ ♦ ♦ ♦ ♦

The Big Picture
Some Final Thoughts

Humankind has not woven the web of life. We are but one thread within it. Whatever we do to the web, we do to ourselves. All things are bound together. All things connect. *Chief Seattle*

It has been more than a decade since that fateful day in Russia. Things have changed, externally and internally. In the same way that the wall dividing East and West Berlin was breached and destroyed, the wall between my intellect and my heart dissolved and the pain vanished.

The first feelings of relief came with the momentous discovery that I could get rid of emotional distress, no matter how painful, no matter how long I had suffered, no matter how deep the hurt, no matter how many other things I had tried. That it can be gotten rid of quickly, easily, naturally, and without medication. That the solution is always at hand, available at a moment's notice. That it is free of charge and requires no one else's cooperation.

This discovery comes in waves. The first is intellectual, just knowing that there is a way to do it.

> *I was so on edge and depressed and anxiety ridden before the class that I was really anxious to fix whatever the problem was, and I started looking forward to that opportunity, to finding out what was eating at me and going through the process. I was looking forward to it tremendously.*

> *Though I was fearful before the process, I knew that I needed to get this out. I knew that once I got it out I would feel better.*

The second comes immediately after the first explosion

> *It was between feeling almost numb and almost in a twilight zone, but euphoria at the same time. I felt a lot lighter, and it made me feel good.*

> *I feel like I've released Niagara Falls. It's been an exhausting journey, but it feels so good to rest.*

> *I was in a wordless state. I don't understand it still. But the main point is that something was lifted and I feel better. I feel a lot better now.*

The third comes within days or weeks and the dawning comprehension that the relief has been broad and deep.

> *I was pretty much lazy. My usual obsessive compulsive disorder wasn't there. I just felt like I didn't need to dust, I just wanted to relax. I have less stress, less anxiety dealing*

with people now. Things that I got out just don't bother me any more.

I can't believe what was in there. How deep and painful it was. How much it affected my everyday life without my knowing it. I feel like something is gone. Like the poison was ejected. I am actually looking forward to the next time, believe it or not. Every day is easier than it was before. And as I do this in the future, I know that I will be that much more serene.

But there is more. There is a second emotional revolution, softer and gentler and more subtle than the first. It comes from time to time, when one is in more reflective moods. It happens when one realizes that those things that used to trigger emotional distress no longer do.

When I realized that when people brought up my past relationship it didn't push my buttons, I was tickled pink. It was gone. And when it finally hit me, I jumped around for joy.

A couple of years ago everything would trigger me. If my husband dripped water from the shower it would trigger me. I took everything personally. I felt controlled and trapped. At the slightest drop of a hat, I wanted to run. I was just fearful. Anything would set me off. Wow, I can't even tell you how much more relaxed and calm I am.

It happens when you reflect back and can't remember how long it has been since you were last in emotional turmoil. When you recall with a smile that there was once a time you could not remember the last moment of peace.

Compared to a couple of years ago, I'm so much more at peace, so much happier, so much more settled, so much more in the moment of living.

The third is more an evolution than a revolution. It is even more subtle and elegant, complex and mysterious than the first two. As the stored pain of a tumultuous childhood fades away it leaves in its wake more subtle sensations, an inner world of which one was previously unaware. Like Dorothy who slowly opens the window to find herself in the Land of Oz, a world of brilliant colors and exciting adventures, it is a world that quite naturally evolves and unfolds. It requires no work, no effort, no thinking. The changes are not intellectual, they are visceral. They just come, like a surprising but welcomed and delightful guest and change one's relationship to the external world and to nature forever.

> We've done better by avoiding dragons rather than by slaying them.
> —Warren Buffett

The environment is transformed from the enemy, into a miraculous and invaluable friend.

Pain, in the rare moments that it makes an appearance, becomes a small signal to do something different. Struggle is a sign to go in another direction. Conflict is a message that there is some old emotional memory still inside that is asking to be set free.

> *There was a time when Robert Moses, the man who single-handedly fought the governor, the legislature, the bureaucracy to build the parks of New York, was my hero. But today, Warren Buffet, a man who does not struggle with life has taken his place.*

One's own inner voice gradually gets louder while the voices of others assume a more modulated tone. Setting boundaries, is automatic, not something to think about or ponder.

> *I am more direct, clearer about who I am, more honest, less frightened of others. I tell people what I feel. I used to be the nice guy, in order to placate people. I'm more honest now, more straightforward and more me. I'm not afraid of*

other people, not afraid of what they will think. I am comfortable just being me.

When I got back from Russia, it was just three weeks before Christmas. My mother, of course, wanted me to fly to Syracuse for the holiday, but I was drained of energy too tired to make the effort. At one time, I might have made an excuse, a major project, a graduate exam, but this time, without even thinking about it, I just told her no. I wasn't angry with her, I said. I wasn't resentful, I was just dealing with some childhood stuff and didn't have any energy left over. And, for the first time, no matter what she said, I didn't feel guilty.

It is the emotional release, not hours of "thinking about your issues" that produces true insight.

Real insight flows into your life as a result of "going to the center of the pain" as a result of the old stuff coming up and out. It takes no thinking, no intellectual effort.

> *My past relationship was an exact copy of my relationship with my mother. He drank, she drank, he took pills, she took pills, he was out of control, she was out of control. I felt frightened and vulnerable and in charge with them both. It hit me even though I wasn't even thinking about it. I mean, I wasn't trying to figure it out at the time. I had been through the process of getting these feelings up and out a couple of weeks earlier, and suddenly I was making very specific connections that had eluded me before.*

Knowledge is more important than information.

Information is data you get from the outside, from experts, from scientists, from others. Knowledge is what happens when you pass that data through your body and note the responses.

I used to make career decisions by getting lots and lots of information, asking my friends what they thought, and I was still unsure of my final choice. The last time, though, I decided to use a different technique. I didn't talk to anyone. I simply got into a quiet place, imagined myself in each of the two jobs I had been offered, and noted how my body reacted. I was definitely more attracted to one alternative than the other, and that's the one I took. I felt so different afterward. I felt sure of my decision, I didn't question myself. It was great and it took a whole lot less time!

In Western industrialized nations, it is traditional to define truth as supported by objective, scientific fact. There is also a tendency to believe that one size fits all. But there is more than one kind of truth. There is not only an external truth, there is an internal truth as well.

Your body's internal responses are a type of truth that cannot be accessed by asking your friends or consulting experts to help you make a decision. It is a type of truth that is essential if you are going to live the life you were intended to live, if you are going to "follow your bliss." When you are reading a book – even this one – or listening to an expert, do you ask only "what data supports this theory?" or do you consult your "gut" to tell you whether or not you are resisting a truth – is it triggering an uncomfortable response? Or, even if it is uncomfortable, is it striking a cord of truth? In the best of all worlds, we would both consult our intellect and our feelings.

The ability to be objective and rational comes as a result not of controlling one's emotions but from letting them go.

As long as the old emotions remain inside, they, not your rational mind control your experiences, the relationships you chose, your life, no matter how hard you try to make it otherwise. The emotional mind is stronger and faster than the rational mind, and Mother Nature is committed to cleaning it out. No matter how much we attempt to control our emotions with our rational minds, no matter how much temporary success we might have, we are doomed to eventual failure. But as soon as the old emotions are cleaned out, as soon as our childhood issues are completed, rationality is automatic, natural. It is the ultimate in growing up.

> *It is amazing how cool I am when everyone around me is loosing their tempers. For the first time, I can back off and analyze what is going on because I am not in the middle of it. None of my buttons is being pushed because I don't have any anymore. It is only since I have given up control that I actually feel in control.*

Trust is not about the other person, it is about oneself.

Trust is knowing you will attract into your life that which you need to become whole. It is knowing that when distressful relationships and painful experiences inhabit your life they are there to help you clean out some old stuff. Trust is knowing that when it is all gone, you will attract only that which fulfills your dreams.

> *I'm not fearful anymore. When I have an issue that I know I need to get rid of, I know I can do it. I know how to do it so it will never bother me again. I am a new person with a whole new perspective on life. I am free, happier, more creative. I'm not a victim anymore.*

Trust is not about "them." We can never control "them." It is about getting rid of our old stuff.

Forgiveness is not a decision

Forgiveness occurs automatically. When the pain is gone, there is nothing left to forgive. No anger, no angst, no anxiety, no pain, no depression, no fear, only tranquility and serenity. Though one may or may not be able to maintain relationships with the persons who "caused" the original pain, they will be forgiven. It is not something one does, it just happens.

Listen to the voices of those who have adopted the cathartic process as a way of life:

> *I felt lighter and carefree. The sun seemed to be shining brighter, smells were more intense, and my body glowed with energy. I felt like kicking up my heels and running. I felt happy. Was it really possible to feel happy after experiencing all that pain and sadness? Evidently it was.*

> *I left feeling surprisingly good after the misery I'd been through. I somehow felt I'd been on a long hike to the top of a mountain. I was coming back home to myself.*

> *When I first "went over the falls," I experienced relief so strong, I almost sat up and cheered. It felt so good to not have to control everything. I felt so free and joyful. Like skipping through life. All the pain is gone now, and I can hardly believe how easy life has become, how stress free. Even my friends have noticed it.*

Emotions are closely allied with the spirit

For those who have been through the process for some time, there is inevitably a depth to life that there never was before. Partly it's the lack of fear, knowing that no matter what happens, pain will never overtake one's life again. Part is the lack of effort, the ability to relax and let life unfold. Part is the joy of knowing that the change is permanent, that it can't be taken away. Part is knowing that the world makes sense. That the pain is not "wrong." That it is instead, part of the healing process, a great and miraculous gift from nature.

For the first time in the lives of many who have suffered, there is the knowledge that they are not alone. No longer must they fight to stay alive. There is a friend inside, a protector, something or someone that will take care of them as long as they listen.

> *Things have evened out in my life, and the problems I have had, well, the solutions come to me more easily than they had, they seem to present themselves to me in a way they didn't before.*

> *There is so much joy now. So much tranquility and ease. I am astounded that it is so easy, and at the depth of the change inside. I feel safe and protected. I know that even if I am not aware of danger intellectually, as long as I keep checking in with my body, with my most subtle feelings, they will keep me away from harm. I am so grateful for the universe, how it is put together, how it works. I have spiritual, and even religious experiences now, something very new for me. I didn't used to even understand other people when they talked about their spiritual feelings. Now they are real for me too.*

And finally, I would like to close with a quote by my friend and author of a wonderful book, *Come Here*, Richard Berendzen. He writes

> *I feel unburdened, free, relaxed, open, alive. My view now has changed about myself and about others. Without sounding too grand about it, I seem now both to "think" and to "feel." And in a surprising way, I sense other people's challenges, often long before they tell me about them. In an equally surprising fashion, people have come to talk to me – men and woman, friends and strangers. They have shared with me things in their own lives they say they've never told anyone before. Somehow they sense that I'll understand, that I'm a "safe harbor" for them.*

In short, it has been a remarkable journey. One filled with difficulty and pain, but also renewal and hope. The journey never ends, but the rewards don't either. Freedom and openness have no equals."

The only thing I can add is amen

Resources

◆ ◆ ◆ ◆ ◆

Books

Alexander, Theresa Sheppard. *Facing the Wolf: Inside the Process of Deep Feeling Therapy.* E. P. Dutton, April, 1997

Arterburn, Stephen; Felton, Jack. *Toxic Faith.* Harold Shaw, Publishers. February, 2001

Appignanesi, Lisa and Forrester, John. *Freud's Women.* Other Press, September, 2001

Athens, Lonnie. *The Creation of Dangerous, Violent Criminals.* University of Illinois Press, October, 1992

Bass, Ellen; Davis, Laura; *The Courage to Heal.* Harper Perennial, July, 1994

Beattie, Melody. *The Language of Letting Go.* Hazelton, July, 1996.

Berendzen, Richard. *Come Here.* Villard Books, New York, 1993

Beutler, Larry. *Am I Crazy or Is It My Shrink.* Oxford University Press, April, 1998.

Blumenson, Martin. *The Patton Papers.* Houghton Mifflin, 1972-74.

Breggin, Peter. *Your Drug May Be Your Problem: How and Why to Stop Taking Psychiatric Medications.* Perseus, August, 2000.

Breggin, Peter. *Prozac: Panacea or Pandora? the Rest of the Story on the New Class of SSRI Antidepressants Prozac, Zoloft, Paxil, Lovan, Luvox & More.* Cassia Publications, June 1994.

Breggin, Peter and Breggin, Ginger. *The War Against Children.* St. Martin's Press, September 1994

Brand, Paul. *The Gift Nobody Wants.* Harper Perennial, 1988.

Brown, Barbara. *Stress and the Art of Biofeedback.* Harper Collins, January, 1977.

Buffett, Warren. *Thoughts of Chairman Buffett : Thirty Years of Unconventional Wisdom From the Sage of Omaha.* Harper Business, 1998.

Buffett, Warren. *Warren Buffett Speaks : Wit And Wisdom From The World's Greatest Investor.* New York : Wiley, 1997.

Campbell, Terence. *Beware the Talking Cure.* Social Issues Resources Series, September, 1994

Catherall, Don R. *Back from the Brink: A Family Guide to Overcoming Traumatic Stress.* Bantam Doubleday. June, 1992

Cousins, Norman. *The Healing Heart: Antidotes To Panic And Helplessness* G.K. Hall, Boston, 1984.

Cousins, Norman. *Anatomy of an Illness as Perceived by the Patient : Reflections On Healing And Regeneration.* W. Norton, N. Y., 1979

Deberry, Stephen. *The Externalization of Consciousness and the Psychopathology of Everyday Life.* Greenwood Publishing Group, March 1991.

Deberry, Stephen. *Quantum Psychology: Steps to a Postmodern Ecology of Being.* Praeger Pub Text, February, 1993.

Edwards, Larry. *Buster, A Legend in Laughter.* McGuinn and McGuire, 1995

Engel, Beverly. *Loving Him without Losing You: How to Stop Disappearing and Start Being Yourself.* John Wiley and Sons, January 2001

Hock, Dee *Birth of the Chaordic Age.* Berrett-Koehler Publishers. 1999.

Frattaroli, Elio. *Healing the Soul in the Age of the Brain: Becoming Conscious in an Unconscious World.* Viking Press, September, 2001.

Gazzaniga, Michael. *Nature's Mind : The Biological Roots Of Thinking, Emotions, Sexuality, Language, And Intelligence*, BasicBooks, N. Y., 1992.

Gazzaniga, Michael. *The Mind's Past.* University of California Press, 1998.

Glenmullen, Joseph. *Prozac Backlash : Overcoming the Dangers of Prozac, Zoloft, Paxil, and Other Antidepressants with Safe, Effective Alternatives.* Simon and Schuster, March 2000.

Goleman, Daniel. *Emotional Intelligence.* Bantam Books, July 1997

Goleman, Daniel. *Vital Lies, Simple Truths: The Psychology of Self-Deception.* Touchstone Books, January, 1996

Gray, John. *What You Can Feel, You Can Heal: A Guide to Enriching Relationships.* Heart Publishing Company, 1984

Hillman, James. *We've Had A Hundred Years of Psychotherapy and the World's Getting Worse.* Harper San Francisco, May, 1993

Horgan, John. *The Undiscovered Mind: How the Human Brain Defies Replication, Medication and Explanation.* Free Press, September 1999.

Janov, Arthur. *The New Primal Scream.* Trafalger Square, May, 2000

Jensen, Jean. *Reclaiming Your Life*: *A Step-By-Step Guide to Using Regression Therapy to Overcome the Effects of Childhood Abuse.* Plume. October 1996

LeDoux, Joseph. *The Emotional Brain: The Mysterious Underpinnings of Emotional Life.* Touchstone Books, March, 1998.

Le Doux, Joseph. *The Synaptic Self: How Our Brains Become Who We Are.* Penguin Group, 2002

Leshan, Lawrence. *The Dilemma of Psychology: A Psychologist Looks at His Troubled Profession.* E. P. Dutton, November, 1990.

Lowenstein, Roger. *Buffett : The Making Of An American Capitalist.* Random House, 1995.

Lutz, Tom. *Crying: The Natural and Cultural History of Tears.* Tom Lutz. W.W. Norton, 1999.

Maeder, Thomas. *Children of Psychiatrists and Other Psychotherapists.* Harper Collins, January, 1989.

Meade, Marion. *Buster Keaton: Cut to the Chase.* Harper Collins, 1995

Miller, Alice. *Drama of the Gifted Child.* Basic Books, December, 1996

Mithers, Carol Lynn. *Therapy Gone Mad.* Persus Books, April 1994

Norden, Michael. *Beyond Prozac: Brain-Toxic Lifestyles, Natural Antidotes, and New Generation Antidepressants.* Harper-Collins, October, 1996

Nyberg, David. *The Varnished Truth: Truth Telling and Deceiving in Ordinary Life.* University of Chicago Press, November, 1994

Niehoff, Debra. *The Biology of Violence (How Understanding the Brain, Behavior, and Environment Can Break the Vicious Circle of Aggression).* Free Press, January, 1999.

Oz, Mehmet, *Healing From The Heart : A Leading Heart Surgeon Explores The Power Of Complementary Medicine.* Dutton, New York, 1998

Pelletier, Kenneth. *Mind as Healer, Mind as Slayer: A Holistic Approach to Healing Stress Disorders.* Delta, August, 1992

Pert, Candace. *Molecules of Emotion.* Simon and Schuster, February, 1999.

Revel, Jean-Francois. The *Flight from Truth: The Reign of Deceit in the Age of Information.* Random House, January, 1992

Robbins, Alexandra; Wilner, Abby. *Quarterlife Crisis: The Unique Challenges of Life in Your Twenties.* J. P. Tarchner/Putnam, N. Y., 2001

Sarno, John MD, *The Mindbody Prescription: Healing the Body, Healing the Pain.* Time Warner, 19998

Schaef, Ann Wilson. *Co-dependence, Misunderstood, Mistreated.* Harper San Francisco, January, 1992

Solter, Alethea. *Tears and Tantrums: What to Do When Babies and Children Cry.* Shining Star Press,

Stettbacher, J. Konrad. *Making Sense of Suffering: The Healing Confrontation With Your Own Past.* Merit Pub International, September, 1993

Stone, Tom. *Cure by Crying.* Cure by Crying Inc. March 1997

Sylvester, Robert. *A Celebration of Neurons: An Educator's Guide to the Human Brain.* Association for Supervision & Curriculum Development. July 1995.

Wade, Nicholas, Editor. *The Science Times Book of the Brain.* Lyons Press, June, 1998.

Wiener, Daniel. *Albert Ellis: Passionate Skeptic.* Praeger Publishers, 1988

Williams, Redford and Williams, *Anger Kills.* Harper Mass Market Publications, December, 1998.

Zilbergeld, Bernie. *The Shrinking of America: Myths of Psychological Change.* Little Brown & Company, March 1983

Zohar, Danah. *SQ: Connecting with our Spiritual Intelligence.* Bloomsbury Pub Plc, January, 2001

Zohar, Danah and Marshall, Ian. *The Quantum Society: Mind, Physics, and a New Social Vision. William Morrow and Company,* March 1994

Zohar, Danah. *Rewiring the Corporate Brain: Using the New Science to Rethink How We Structure and Lead Organizations.* Berrett Kohler Pub, November, 1997.

Zohar, Danah. *Quantum Self: Human Nature and Consciousness Defined by the New Physics.* Quill, May 1991

Zukav, Gary. *The Dancing Wu Li Masters.* Quill, New York, 1979

Zukav, Gary. *The Seat of the Soul.* Fireside Press. New York, 1989.

Magazines, Journals, Newspapers and Pamphlets

American Association of Suicidology

American Diabetes Association

American Psychiatric Association Monitor

American Psychological Association

Arthritis Foundation

Begley, Sharon. Religion and the Brain. *Newsweek,* May 7, 2001.

Boss, S. J. The Write Cure for Stress. *Good Housekeeping,* September, 1999.

Brain-Injury Victims Can Spot Liars. *Arizona Republic,* May 11, 2000.

Brody, Jane. Help for Cybersex Addiction. *New York Times,*

Center for Disease Control US Crime Statistics

Clinical Psychiatric News

Cohen, Sheldon; Frank, Ellen; Doyle, William J.; Skoner, David P.; Rabin, Bruce; and Gwaltney, Jack M., Jr., (1998) Types Of Stressors That Increase Susceptibility To The Common Cold In Healthy Adults. *Health Psychology,* 17, 214-223.

Elias, Marilyn. Aerobic Exercise Eases Depression, Study Finds. *Gannett News Service.*

Funk, Joel. Naturopathic and Allopathic Healing A Developmental Comparison. June, 1994.

Gorman, Christine. The Science of Anxiety. *Time Magazine,* June 10, 2002. Gross, J.J., & Levenson, R. W. (1997) Hiding Feelings: The Acute Effects Of Inhibiting Negative And Positive Emotion. *Journal of Abnormal Psychology,* 106, 95-103.Jorgensen, R. S., Johnson, B. T., Kolodziej, M. E., & Schreer, G. E. (1996) Elevated Blood Pressure And Personality: A Meta-Analytic Review. *Psychological Bulletin,* 120, 293-320.

Kantrowitz, Barbara. In Search Of Sleep. *Newsweek,* July 15, 2002.

Hunt, Morton. Navagating the Therapy Maze: A Consumer's Guide To Mental Health Treatment. *New York Times*

Journal of Consulting and Clinical Psychology, 1994

Kempermann, Gerd; Gage, Fred. New Nerve Cells for the Adult Brain. *Scientific American*, May, 1999.

Kirsch, Irving. Listening to Prozac but Hearing Placebo: A Meta-analysis of Antidepressant Medication. *Prevention and Treatment,* 1998

Klein, Kitty. Keep a Diary, Reap Cognitive Rewards. *Psychology Today.* March/April, 2002.

Lerner, Mary. Facing Your Fear. *Parade Magazine.* 2002

McClam, Erin. Cybersex: It's a Growing Epidemic. *Arizona Republic.*

Mulrine, Anna. Where do hopes go? Teen suicide is a national tragedy. Here's on town's story. *U. S. News and World Report*, May 7, 2001.

Nader, K., Schafe, G. and LeDoux, J.E. (2000) Fear Memories Require Protein Synthesis In The Amygdala For Reconsolidation After Retrieval. *Nature*, Aug 17 406(6797):722-6.

National Association for Mental Illness

National Center on Sleep Disorders

National Institute of Mental Health/Practice Directorate

Newsweek, March 18, 1998

Newsweek. *In Search of Sleep.* July 15, 2002

New York Times, June 30, 2002

Noonan, David and Cowley, Geoffrey. Prozac vs. Placebos. *Newsweek*, July 15, 2002.

Ohman, Arne; Esteves, Francisco, Flykt, Anders. Isolating the Enemy: How We Find Threats Fast. *Psychology Today.* January/February, 2002.

Psychiatric News

Perspective: A Mental Health Magazine

Peterson, Karen. Distrust Grows Dramatically In Young Adults, Survey Says. *USA Today.*

PsycPort: The Who Report on Culture, Society and Depression

Report by Joseph Califano

Ritalin May Cause Long-Lasting Changes in Brain-Cell Function, University of Buffalo. *Science Daily*, November 12, 2001

Teicher, Martin. Scars that won't heal: the neurobiology of child abuse. *Scientific American*, March 2002.

Schafe, G.E., Nadel, N.V., Sullivan, G.M., Harris, A., LeDoux, J.E. (1999) Memory consolidatoin for contextual and auditory fear conditioning is dependent on protein synthesis, PKA, and MAPkinase. *Learning & Memory* 6:97-110.

School Shooters Present Signs Long Before Action. *Arizona Republic.* October 15, 2000.

Shim, Paul and Shim, Saran. The Daddy Dividend. *Psychology Today.* March/April, 2002.

Shock Therapy Has High Relapse Rate. Arizona Republic

Tired? Well, join the crowd. *Arizona Republic*, March 28, 2001.

United States Department of Health and Human Services

United States Center for Disease Control

Weh, Patricia. Too Many Tasks Rattles Brain. *Arizona Republic*, Sunday, May 28, 2000.

Websites

Society for Neuroscience http://web.sfn.org/

Amygdala: the amazing brain music adventure http://viewzone.com/amygdala/

Dept of Psychiatry, Washington Univ. http://biopsychiatry.com/amygdala.html

NIDA http://www.nida.nih.gov/NIDA_Notes/NNVol11N3/Amygdala.html

Health/Emotions Research Institute, U of Wisc. http://www.healthemotions.org/

T. D. Lingo Homepage http://www.brainbomb.org/
University of Wisconsin http://www.anatomy.wisc.edu/coro97/s/C4.HTM
Anxieties.com http://anxieties.com/
Anxiety Disorders Association of America http://www.adaa.org/
Nat. Assoc. for Mental Health http://www.nami.org/helpline/anxiety9909.html
Medline Plus http://www.nlm.nih.gov/medlineplus/phobias.html
Journal of Personality and Social Psych. http://www.cognitivetherapy.com/anger.html
The CBT Website http://www.cognitivetherapy.com/outlinks.html
Center for Cognitive/Behavioral Therapy http://www.hope4ocd.com/
Internet Encyclopedia of Philosophy http://www.utm.edu/research/iep/
Philosophy News Service http://www.philosophynews.com/
Readings in Modern Philosophy http://www.ets.uidaho.edu/mickelsen/readings.htm
The Big View http://www.thebigview.com/
Slate Magazine http://slate.msn.com/
Eric Database http://askeric.org/Eric/
Bibliomania http://www.bibliomania.com/
Library of Congress http://www.loc.gov/
Library Spot http://www.libraryspot.com/
PBS http://www.pbs.org/neighborhoods/history/
Time Magazine http://www.time.com/time/time100/
Lives, the Biography Resource http://amillionlives.com/
Forbes http://www.forbes.com/2001/09/27/400.html
American Foreign Policy Council http://afpc.org/
US Securities and Exchange Commission http://www.sec.gov/edgar.shtml
Federal Statistics http://www.sec.gov/edgar.shtml
Biological Psychiatry, Journal of Psychiatric Neuroscience
http://www.sec.gov/edgar.shtml
Junkscience.com http://www.junkscience.com/
Mind and Body http://serendip.brynmawr.edu/Mind/Table.html
Foundation for Human Enrichment http://www.traumahealing.com/
Mental Health Net http://www.mentalhelp.net/
Plymouth State College http://www.plymouth.edu/thirdtier/faculty_member
Danah Zohar http://www.dzohar.com/home.htm
Bright Life http://www.fearintopower.com/
Journal of the American Medical Association http://pubsearch.ama-assn.org/search
The Psychedelic Library http://www.druglibrary.org/schaffer/lsd/grof.htm
Healthy Awareness Network http://www.healthyawareness.com/
US Public Health Serv. http://www.surgeongeneral.gov/library/mentalhealth/home.html
The Age of Anxiety http://mars.wnec.edu/~grempel/courses/wc2/lectures/anxiety.html
A Talk with Joseph LeDoux http://www.edge.org/3rd_culture/ledoux/ledoux_p2.html
LeDoux Lab http://www.cns.nyu.edu/home/ledoux/
Psychiatric Drug Facts http://www.breggin.com/
Psychology of Religion http://psychwww.com/psyrelig/
The Association for Humanistic Psychology http://ahpweb.org/aboutahp/whatis.html
Mental Health Matters http://www.mental-health-matters.com/
US Center for Mental Health Services http://www.mentalhealth.org/
American Psychology Association http://www.apa.org/
Mental Health Association of Arizona http://mhaaz.com/
American Psychological Society http://www.psychologicalscience.org/
PsychInfo Direct http://psycinfo.apa.org/demo/
NIMH For the Public http://www.nimh.nih.gov/publicat/index.cfm
Useful Links for Psychologists http://www.wku.edu/~kuhlenschmidt/sallink.htm

From Turmoil to Tranquility

Scientific American http://www.sciam.com/0697issue/0697review1.html
ABC News http://more.abcnews.go.com/sections/living/inyourhead/allinyourhead
Salon Magazine http://www.salon.com/books/log/1999/08/31/unabomber/index.html
CNN/Time http://www.cnn.com/SPECIALS/1997/unabomb/
Codependency Information and More http://epinions.henderco.com/index.htm
APA Press Release http://www.apa.org/releases/catharsis.html
Newsweek http://www.msnbc.com/news/NW-front_Front.asp
Frontline http://www.pbs.org/wgbh/pages/frontline/shows/nature/
The Universe as a Hologram http://www.crystalinks.com/holographic.html
Holodynamic Compression http://www.maui.net/~shaw/celes/dcmind.html
Principia Cybernetica http://pespmc1.vub.ac.be/SYSTHEOR.html
4 Addictions.com http://4addictions.4anything.com/4/0,1001,1240,00.html
Dr. Koop http://www.drkoop.com/wellness/mental_health/sexual_addiction/sexaddict.
ABC News http://abcnews.go.com/onair/2020/2020_000621_prozac_feature.html
Existentialism http://members.aol.com/KatharenaE/private/Philo/philo.html
The Myth http://dharma-haven.org/science/myth-of-scientific-method.htm
Key Contemporary Thinkers http://acnet.pratt.edu/~arch543p/help/Freud.html
Internet Encyclopaedia of Philosophy http://www.utm.edu/research/iep/l/locke.htm
Knowledge http://mail.aristotle.net/knowledge/edulink.html
NY Times http://www.nytimes.com/library/national/science/health/080800hth-behavior-culture.html
The Sacramento Bee http://www.unabombertrial.com/archive/1996/041196-5.html
The Scourge of Prozac http://cat007.com/prozac.htm
Family Education Network http://www.familyeducation.com/article/0,1120,2-7411-0-3,00.html
Cults http://www.rickross.com/
Frontline http://www.pbs.org/wgbh/pages/frontline/shows/kinkel/
Self-Help Magazine http://www.shpm.com/articles/child_behavior/cfviol.html
Psychotropic Drugs and Kids http://neuro-www.mgh.harvard.edu/forum
_2/OCDF/6.26.995.34PMPsychotropic.html
Chaos Forum http://www.chaosforum.com/
Where the Money Goes http://netec.wustl.edu/WoPEc/data/Papers/nbrnberwo5294.html
Drugs and Anxiety http://salmon.psy.plym.ac.uk/year2/psy221anxiety/psy221anxiety.htm
Biology of Emotional Disorders http://pages.nyu.edu/~er26/depression.html
Raising Children/Uncivil Society http://www.city-journal.org/html/7_3_raising.html
Dope on Drugs http://www.american.edu/academic.depts/spa/justice/publications/post.
Brain Source http://www.brainsource.com/
Stress and Illness http://www.stressillness.com/
Psych Immune System? http://cogprints.soton.ac.uk/documents/disk0/00/00/11/47/
ADHD, Drug Free http://www.caer.com/

About the Author

♦ ♦ ♦ ♦ ♦

Cindy Cooke is a community college psychology professor in Arizona, teaches self-help seminars nationally, and is an expert on the causes of and cures for Amygdala Deficit Disorder, a syndrome that lies at the heart of the growing epidemic of emotional distress. She is the former Executive Director of the World Affairs Council and the California Democratic Leadership Council. She has a bachelors degree in psychology and a masters in adult education, and has done post graduate work in organizational development at Pepperdine University in Malibu. In 1979, she was named an Outstanding Young Woman in America, and is a sought-after speaker in the field of personal development.

The illegitimate daughter of an Arizona-born lawyer and congressman, Cooke spent her first several years hidden away in a series of private foster homes. Though she joined her parents at the age of seven, and lived with them for eleven years, her father continued to live a double life until his death at the age of 82 and never publicly acknowledged her.

The consequences of these tenuous beginnings included a hand-washing fetish at the age of 4, an early and difficult marriage in her teens, debilitating panic attacks, and an unending plague of life crises as an adult. Finally, while on a personal trip to Russia in the early 90's, Cooke experienced a cathartic experience and a profound paradigm shift that turned all of what she thought she knew about psychology inside out.

For the last 10 years, Cooke has studied the latest brain research and pursued answers to why, despite years of therapy she had not "gotten it" before the crisis in Russia. This book is the result of her research and her work with others who have suffered and recovered from extreme anxiety, anger, depression, and life crises.

Order Form

Cindy Cooke
invites you to introduce the
Turmoil to Tranquility philosophy
to a friend with a
book, audio tape or CD

Book ($18.95 each)   **Number of copies____**
5 Audio Tapes ($49.95)   **Number of copies____**
5 CD's ($49.95)   **Number of copies____**
**❏Please add me to your newsletter e-mail list
and let me know about upcoming seminars.
(e-mail address: _____)**

Enclosed is: $___ (Add $5 for shipping and handling.)
Name: _____
Address: _____
City:_____State_____Zip_____
MC/VISA/Discover/AMEX:_____
Exp. Date:_____ Signature:_____

Mail to 9699 North Hayden Road, Suite108, Scottsdale, AZ 85258;
call 480 36PEACE; or order online at TherapistWithin.com